PREACH WOMAN PREACH

My Preaching Journey

PREACH WOMAN PREACH

Rita Twiggs Ministries, Inc.
P. O. Box 64223
Washington, DC 20029
www.ritatwiggs.org

VIP PUBLISHING
3758 S. Carrier Parkway, Suite 108
Grand Prairie, Texas 75052

ISBN: 0-9754407-05

Preach Woman Preach: My preaching Journey/Rita L. Twiggs

1. Christian Life 2. Ministry Life

Printed in the United States of America
10 9 8 7 6 5 4 3 2 1

ALSO BY RITA L. TWIGGS
LOOSED TO LOVE

DEDICATION

This book is dedicated to my darling mother, Pearl Elizabeth Mosley, who pushed me out into this world in 1951, and has gently continued to push me with her love, patience, prayers, faith, and encouragement my whole life. I am her first born, and so very proud to be her child. Mom, you are my hero, and the wind beneath my wings. I love you so much!

I also dedicate this work to my wonderful father, Virgil Mosley, for his loving protection, unselfish provision and wise counsel. Through him, God has continued to show me His love as a Father. Thanks for letting the Lord use you Dad, I love you!

Finally, I dedicate this book to the memory of my precious grandmother, Jewel Dixon, my hilariously funny aunt Florence, and my warrior cousin Debbie, who are all with the Lord. Their wisdom, wit and courage have become ever-appreciating assets in my life!

ACKNOWLEDGEMENTS

My heartfelt gratitude goes to Frances L. Anthony, my dearest friend, who has always encouraged me in my dreams and visions no matter how crazy they may have sounded. I bless God for you, Frances. Thank you for believing God with me, and praying me through, time and time again!

Thank you Sandra L. Jackson, Esq., for being the vessel of honor that the Lord used to instigate, and facilitate the writing of this book. The Lord bless you Dr., for provoking me to finish this good work.

To my sisters, brothers, cousins, aunts, uncles, nieces, nephews, and everyone else who claims me as being related, I am blessed above measure to have you all as a part of the fabric of my life.

To Bishop T.D. Jakes, Sr., First Lady Serita A. Jakes, and the Potter's House Church family, I thank God for your love and support that has added new dimensions to my life and ministry.

Finally, I thank God for the countless number of brothers and sisters in Christ who have encouraged me in this endeavor, and say to the team of publishing miracle workers who lovingly, and patiently, helped me to birth this book— Teneka, Stephanie, LeRonn, may God's choicest blessings be yours always.

CONTENTS

PREFACE

To the Reader:

Over the years, I have had the privilege of training numerous young people who were aspiring to be preachers. For the most part, that training has been through the vehicles of teaching or preaching, and one-on-one counseling sessions. At times I have taught about ministry and its' dynamics, or discussed personal issues related to being in ministry. These discussions were usually initiated to answer questions or bring clarity to an issue, although I have also used them to challenge and correct students God has placed in my charge.

In addition I have listened to, observed, and often sought to edify both men and women in ministry who were overwhelmed with their God-given assignment. Being in ministry is never easy, and all of us need encouragement from time to time. My sincere desire has been to encourage young ministers to focus on their relationship with the Lord, because out of this is effective ministry birthed. I believe, and have always taught, that preaching must be done with the intent of leading men and women to a saving knowledge of Jesus Christ, and a relationship with the Father through Him. Today, I am as committed to this truth as I was over twenty-five years ago.

In 1978, as a beginning evangelist, I was convinced of the Word of God, which teaches that he who wins souls is wise. Today, as a pastor and teacher my heart is still evangelistic. I yet preach to win souls! But, now more than ever, I strive to minister the Word of God with accuracy to those I am privileged to counsel or teach. In past years I recall sessions where young men and women have pulled upon the anointing that the Lord has placed on my life, and golden nuggets of wisdom and experience have been released into their souls. In recent days, however, I have anguished over the fact that these discussions were not recorded. Why the anguish? Perhaps because I believe that transcripts of these sessions would be useful for others who are entering into or growing in ministry. But most especially because I now know how impossible it is to recreate, at will, an environment that would foster such anointed times of personal sharing. As an alternative, the best I could hope to do would be to recall, with God's help, as many of the insights that I gained through those precious experiences as possible, and to record them quickly for future reference!

Thus, it seemed good to the Holy Ghost, and to me also, to take pen in hand and write about some of the experiences I have had, and the knowledge I have gained in these years of ministry. My hope, beloved, is that as you read this book, you will be inspired, challenged, and encouraged concerning this holy thing called preaching; this privileged work called ministry; and above all, this wonderful savior called Jesus Christ! Expect an enlightening, sometimes humorous, and yet sobering journey, as you travel with me through the years of my life that are on its pages. But more than that, as you read, earnestly expect to hear the wonder-filled voice of our God!

Released as an eternal deposit from my life to yours,

Dr. Rita L. Twiggs

CHAPTER 1

THE CALL TO PREACH

Two of the questions most frequently asked of me are: Should a woman preach? How did I know I was called to preach? Let me address question one by saying that no true disciple of Jesus Christ is exempt from the great commission He gave His first disciples in *Matthew 28* and *Mark 17*. Both compelling commands leave no room for debate or delay, and our obedience should be motivated by the love we have for Him. Gospel preaching is, after all, the simple sincere proclamation of the birth, life, death, burial, resurrection and ascension of Jesus the Christ as 'good news' for all mankind! Everybody needs to know the truth of who Jesus is, and preaching is how they will hear and believe it. So, in a very real sense, whether male or female, as believers we are all 'called' into a relationship with God and commissioned by

Him to proclaim His great love! It is reasonable to say then that as we go from day to day, no matter what our gender, our agenda should include the preaching of the gospel as each opportunity is recognized.

The second question however, speaks to me more specifically concerning the God-given assignment that focuses on preaching as a primary vocation. Like any God-given assignment, such as being a doctor, lawyer, teacher, musician, or other profession, it is absolutely essential, whether male or female, to be sure that God has assigned that work to your hand. So, how did I know that God had called me to the vocation of preaching? Let me begin by saying that there were no lightening flashes or claps of thunder or special visions that I can recall. However, early in my life, I believed the Lord had something special for me to do. This is my story, and it is what it is...

IN THE BEGINNING

I remember asking the Lord Jesus Christ to come into my heart at five years of age. Today, I believe with that same heart, that His call to preach was upon me even then. I recall singing an old hymn that my grandmother taught me entitled 'The Old Rugged Cross'. The only verse I sang was:

> *"On a hill far away stood an old rugged cross, the emblem of suffering and shame. But I love that old*

cross where the dearest and best for a world of lost sinners was slain. So I'll cherish the old rugged cross 'til my trophies at last I lay down. I will cling to the old rugged cross and exchange it one day for a crown!" George Bennard, 1913.

I cried through the whole song because it touched my heart so. And, that was for a kindergarten program! Then, at ages six and seven, I started doing religious speeches for church plays. I recall feeling and acting as if I were the only one on stage. I felt the whole audience was mine to command. In addition, I can remember believing with all my heart that every word I spoke from the Bible or about the Lord was meant to come out of my mouth. People were supposed to listen to me! I know that may sound strange, but it is the truth. Whether I was playing Moses, or the Angel Gabriel, or Mary, or Joseph, or Queen Esther, although I was a child, every line was spoken with the thought that I was representing the Lord.

Now, don't get me wrong. I didn't think I was a preacher. Nobody told me I was a preacher. No one prophesied that I would be a preacher. In the beginning, the Lord gave me no special visitation or announcement. I just knew that whenever I spoke anything from or about the Word of God, I felt a strange feeling come over me. I didn't know exactly what it was then, but I experienced a connection to

God that was very real. I know now that it was His Hand upon me. Yes, He just quietly touched me. Afterwards, I had a great hunger for an understanding of God's Word, and I had a strong desire to repeat His Word to others, that would not go away. In retrospect, this must have been the time when I first began to recognize the call of God on my life.

GOING FORWARD

As I got older, my classmates began to see that there was something different about me. At age ten, my friends began to tease me and call me 'the preacher'. My teachers would even ask me to pray or lead devotions —that is, back when devotions were allowed in public schools. I was very comfortable doing these things, even though I was still quite young. In one sense I felt like a 'sore thumb' sticking out among the other students, but in another sense I absolutely loved doing whatever was asked of me. In fact, I loved it so much, I began to volunteer for any opportunity that would allow me to represent the Lord. I always believed from the beginning of my salvation that I was destined to speak concerning the things of God. If that weren't enough, I also thought everyone should believe what I said, because I believed it. I believed it then. I believe it even more now. Looking back, I am convinced that my destiny was calling me, and *that* destiny was to preach the Gospel of Jesus Christ!

MY PLANS OR HIS?

In spite of what I was feeling about speaking for the Lord, as I got older, I began to focus more and more on music in my educational studies. Truth is, I loved music. I played flute, participated in the elementary school choir, and delighted in every moment of playing and singing. By the time I entered junior high school at age twelve, my sights were set on becoming a composer and an orchestral conductor. I wanted to study music in New York and become the resident conductor of the National Symphony Orchestra in Washington D.C. I sang and played the flute, in school and in church, with these plans in my mind. All through high school, becoming a musician was my focus.

At nineteen, I traveled abroad with my family in 1970 and returned to America in 1972. I secured a full time job working at the National Academy of Sciences in computer technology, but music still had first priority in my plans. I attended the University of the District of Columbia and worked diligently toward a degree in music. I still found that whether I was at work, or in school, or in church, or even at home, I was singled out and called upon to pray or have something to `say' for the Lord.

For any special occasion, my family would look to me as the spokesperson for the Lord. At school I prayed for special programs. At work I prayed to open meetings, or said 'grace' at the office parties. Sometimes in church, I would be minding my own business, just sitting in service. Then, more times than I can remember, I would be called upon without warning to 'give remarks'. That is, to stand up and talk about what I had gleaned from the service, or to add any thoughts I might have concerning what had been said or done. Even though many of these opportunities came as a surprise to me, God always had me prepared. I believe this was a part of God's purpose and training for me. He always gave me something to 'say', along with a strong feeling that I was 'saying it' for Him. I understood later that He was just continuing to confirm His plans for me in my mind and heart.

As time went on, giving 'remarks' led to many other requests for me to speak in additional places. By this time, at age twenty-one, I was too old to be doing recitations or parts in plays. Instead, I began to prepare what I called "Faith Speeches" for the Lord, just in case one might be requested of me. For example, I would pick a subject, find scriptures that supported it, and then write what the Bible said about it. This required reading many related scriptures, and researching the subject (topic), using other reference materials like dictionaries, Bible handbooks, and commentaries. Sometimes, my bed would be covered with books, maps, and charts, which were like silent teachers, helping me put together my speech.

If I read a passage of scripture, and a subject came into my mind, I would jot down the subject and write whatever I discovered through continued reading and study. Afterwards, I put the speech in a notebook, fully expecting an opportunity to 'give the speech'. I was prepared by 'faith', and as God allowed opportunities to be presented, I was as happy as a lark to give my 'speech'. Now, this 'giving speeches' went on from place to place for approximately four years.

THE MARK

At the ripe old age of twenty-five, one day two of my male friends, Lyford Banks and James Wilson, who are successful pastors today, were having a conversation about me that I overheard. One said to the other, "she has the mark doesn't she?" The answer came back "sure does"! Of course, I had to interrupt the conversation right away because I wanted to know what 'mark' they were talking about. The only 'mark' I had heard of was the mark of the beast in Revelation —and that wasn't good! When I asked, they laughed and said that they were referring in their own way to the fact that everything about me seemed to say `Preacher', `Preacher', `Preacher'!

Well, needless to say, that conversation called my spirit to attention in a new and entirely different way. I knew I felt "something special" while giving my speeches, but to have somebody who was already a preacher label that `something' in me as `preacher', was completely different. I eventually discovered that I needed only God's command to go, but a part of me was very grateful that He had let someone else see what He was doing. Through this encounter with my brothers, I began to feel as though a different level of accountability had been placed upon me.

Having received the testimony of these two men as further confirmation of God's call on my life, I continued to `speak' whenever He provided the opportunity. I remember the excitement of being asked to present a Bible lesson summary for a Baptist Youth Convention at Princeton University. I was given thirty minutes to teach. The Lord helped me prepare, and many young people indicated what a blessing they had received. In addition, I received many invitations to speak in services where more than one speaker would go forth with an allotted amount of time. This is what was called a `platform' service. Although I shared the platform with others, I counted it a great privilege to have been asked to speak at all. As God saw my faithfulness and obedience in these services, He allowed me to receive more and more invitations to speak 'alone' for other special church services. At this point, I felt an even greater sense of responsibility to study God's Word and prepare 'accurate' speeches. I studied all the time. Finally, I remember praying to God one night and saying, 'God, if You really want me to preach for You, I will, BUT I need You to do three things for me:

1. Give me 'something' to preach!
2. Give me 'somewhere' to preach! And...
3. Please don't let me preach or teach error!

Well, beloved, I know God answers prayers, because of what transpired as soon as I finished praying! Immediately, He confirmed and clarified His calling to me by leading me to *Acts 26:16-18* which says,

> *"But rise, and stand upon thy feet: for I have appeared unto thee for this purpose, to make thee a minister and a witness both of these things which thou hast seen, and of those things in the which I will appear unto thee; Delivering thee from the people, and from the Gentiles, unto whom now I send thee, To open their eyes, and to turn them from darkness to light, and from the power of Satan unto God, that they may receive forgiveness of sins,*

and inheritance among them which are sanctified by faith that is in me."

This was the mandate He had given the apostle Paul, and now He was giving it to Rita. Boy was I humbled. Then, what He did next changed my life forever!

NEVER THE SAME AGAIN

In 1977 at age twenty-six, I was speaking for a Mother's Day "platform" service one Sunday evening. In the middle of talking about my assigned letter "M", out of the clear blue sky I boldly expressed my desire to be filled with the Holy Ghost. That wasn't supposed to be part of the speech! My subject was 'There is More To Being A Mother Than You Think'. I wasn't even thinking about the Holy Ghost. Although I had been raised in the Baptist church, and had spent time studying in the Methodist church, I had never studied about or been filled with the Holy Spirit. (I use Holy Spirit and Holy Ghost interchangeably). So, what caused such an outburst? Well, it started about six months earlier.

One night, a friend of mine named Spurgeon Hawthorne called me. He was so excited that I had to ask him to slow down so I could understand his words. As I listened to him talk about having been filled with the Holy

Ghost, the power and joy I felt coming through his voice over the telephone made me Godly jealous, and even a little angry. Why jealous? Because he had something I knew I didn't have, and it sounded like I really needed it. Why angry? Because no one had ever taught me about being 'filled with the Holy Ghost' *(Acts 1:8).* By then I had read about being filled with the Holy Ghost, but no one I knew had experienced it. Or if they had, no one informed me—that is until my friend told me of his experience over the telephone that night. I could tell by his conversation that this medical doctor, my good friend, had been changed forever by his intimate encounter with the Holy Spirit. Shortly thereafter, he gave up his lucrative medical practice and preached the gospel full time. (A few years later, he joyfully went home to be with the Lord!) That night however, his call provoked me to pursue the same intimate encounter with the Lord he had experienced!

Thus, my earnest desire to be filled with the Holy Ghost came blurting out of me on that fateful Mother's Day. The 'blurting' was not a part of my plans, but it was surely the Lord's will. I say this, because in the service on that Sunday, there sat a little old lady who heard my 'cry', and was used of God to help release me into another dimension of my relationship with Him. Please let me tell you how God filled me with His precious Holy Spirit!

A DIVINE SETUP

Immediately after the Mother's Day service, this little Pentecostal mother and her husband, the pastor, invited me to come and 'speak' to their congregation. The date was set for one month later. It would be a small church in rural Portsmouth, Virginia. It would be a beautiful sunny Sunday morning. It would be a 'Divine setup'!

The pastor had made plans to send a van on Saturday night to pick me up in Washington, D.C. and drive me five hours back to their home in Portsmouth, Virginia. So, that evening, I laid out my most impressive suit (I only owned three). I pressed the matching blouse neatly and laid my shoes, stockings, wig, and everything else I needed on the chair. I just knew I was going to look really sharp. I forgot all about *Proverbs 16:18,* which says, *Pride goeth before destruction, and an haughty spirit before a fall.* With a good bit of vanity stored up in my heart I then proceeded to lie down and take a nap.

When my ride knocked at the door late that night, I arose with a strange spirit of excitement and a bit of disorientation. (I later learned that it is important to be sure you are wide-awake and clear-headed when embarking upon ministry.) I will never be able to explain it, but somehow I crawled up into that van and immediately went back to sleep. Upon arrival five hours later, I wiped the sleep from my eyes, crawled out of the van, and quickly discovered that the only thing I had was the suit. I had no blouse, no shoes, no stockings, and no wig. I felt crushed and humiliated. I ended up borrowing a pair of loafers, and putting my hair in a bun. I also had to borrow some knee high stockings, and a pull over sweater to wear with my suit. Lord, have mercy!

Needless to say, that night vanity and pride were swallowed up, and replaced with a great big dose of humility. I remembered *I Peter 5:5b*, which says, *The Lord resists the proud, and gives grace to the humble.* This humility showed forth in God's simple message of love to His people the following morning. You probably have the revelation by now. Yes, God does have a way of driving vanity out of us, so that He may be glorified. I believe the entire situation was a part of God's plan. He allowed me to forget the things that contributed to my personal vanity. There I was, stripped naked of all arrogance and pride. He humbled me, so that He could make me a blessing to His people, and prepare me for an even greater personal blessing on that day.

Oh, because I have never forgotten that experience, I now dress to impress God, and God alone. I am not trying to look good for people, even though they do see the fruit of my labor (smile). As a footnote, I learned to make a list of the things I need to take with me as I travel, and take time to ensure that everything I need is accounted for through attention to detail.

THE TARRYING SERVICE

I remember the experience as if it were yesterday. There I was in my suit of humility. The congregation warmly received the message of love the Lord had given me from *John 3:16*. I spoke what He told me to say, and one person gave his life to Jesus. I was elated. Then, after the benediction, what took place over the next few hours was a life-changing encounter for me with the Holy Ghost.

After eating Sunday dinner in the fellowship hall, we returned to the sanctuary, and the saints sat me in a chair in the middle of the room. I was about to experience what was known as 'the tarrying service'! It was about five o'clock p.m. The people of God began to pray for me. They encouraged me to praise the Lord. They instructed me concerning the gift of the Holy Ghost, and praised the Lord with and for me about seven hours, until I finally yielded to the Holy Spirit within me. I then began praising God and speaking in tongues as the Spirit of God gave me an utterance.

However, for six hours before this happened I was a hard nut to crack. For me, receiving the infilling of the Holy Ghost was a real challenge, primarily because I was afraid of the "unknown". I didn't know what this 'Holy Ghost' might do to me. At first, I wouldn't say anything, because I thought I would sound silly. Next, I wouldn't lift my hands, because they felt as heavy as lead. As time went on, I became tired, angry and discouraged, because nothing was happening to me. I wanted to give up and go home. I probably would have, BUT GOD! He didn't let the saints give up on me, and He didn't give up on me either! That evening, the people of God prayed for me until I received a release from fear, pride and everything else that had hindered me.

When I finally yielded to the Holy Spirit's moving, I felt it happen. I was saying 'Thank you Jesus', over and over again until I got lost in praise to Him. Then, all of a sudden my mouth felt 'full'—I wanted to speak, but wasn't sure of what to say. When I finally opened my mouth, a little sound like 'teka teka teka' came out. I immediately grabbed my mouth, and the sound stopped. Again I began to say 'Thank you Jesus', and the same thing happened. Well, I knew I wasn't making up the sound that was in my mouth. Every time I would start out saying 'Thank you Jesus', it turned into 'teka teka teka'. It sounded, and felt like baby talk to me, but it melted my heart and made me cry because I knew it wasn't me! The saints began to smile, because they knew that it was the Holy Spirit filling my mouth with the utterance as the scriptures had promised in *(Acts 2:1-4)*. The more I yielded to what I felt in my mouth, the more the Spirit of

God gave me of Himself, until 'teka teka teka' became more sounds and syllables. Eventually these utterances became a river of new words flowing out of my belly, as promised in *John 7:38.*

That night, those caring, patient saints prayed me through to deliverance from pride and fear, and helped me enter into the manifested presence of the Lord for the very first time. I have been speaking in tongues ever since! It took several hours. However, I received all that God gave me that night, and I continue to experience an infilling of the Holy Spirit to this day! Hallelujah!

Now, once I began to speak in tongues, the saints prayed again. This time they prayed that I would not be ashamed or afraid to praise or preach as long as I lived. Likewise, they prayed that I would remain humble for as long as I lived to preach. I thank the Lord for the effectual, fervent prayers of the righteous people of God *(James 5:16b)*. But most of all, I thank my God for filling me with His awesome Holy Spirit! Like my precious friend Spurgeon, since that wonderful Sunday night, my life has never been the same!

FILLED

I believe God filled me with His Holy Spirit in order to open a new dimension of worship, intimacy and revelation of

His divine truth. I knew the 'letter' of the Word (what was written), but He wanted me to know the 'spirit' of the Word (the intent, meaning and application). The Lord really did not want me to preach or teach error. (He remembered my prayer.) I also believe God wanted me to experience this new level of His presence and anointing, because He knew I was going to need it for the rest of my life as I lived for and served Him daily.

With the infilling of the Holy Spirit, I experienced a deeper love and appreciation for God the Father and His Son Jesus Christ. I also felt a stronger determination to live Holy, and preach the good news about Christ to others. His life, His sacrifice, His blood, His name, His love, all of these became more real and much more personal to me after my encounter with His Spirit. The story doesn't end here.

That first night, all night I sang and spoke in tongues. I was so happy, it took hours before I fell asleep on that holy mother's kitchen floor. Then early the next morning when I woke up, I felt clean and new all over. I jumped up off the floor, headed out of the front door of the house and started running with all of my might —in an unfamiliar neighborhood, with no particular destination in mind. As I ran, the sun came beaming beautifully through the treetops, and a fresh morning breeze caressed my face. I could have run on forever. Running up one street and down another, I felt like I had wings. I never tired. I just stopped after about fifteen or twenty minutes. When I stopped, to my surprise, I was standing right in front of a little white wooden church. As I stood there, I remember wondering if I would ever be a pastor. Well, as quickly as the thought came to my mind, it left. I then turned around to try and locate myself. I had no idea where I was. Thankfully, the little Pentecostal mother and her whole family had crowded into the car, and had been following me slowly from behind until I stopped. Boy, was I glad to see them. They took me back to the house and lovingly spoke into my life. Many of the things God gave them to say, were prophecies that are being fulfilled today. Then these precious saints, hugged me, gathered my 'humble' things, and sent me on my way back home —filled and forever changed!

Beloved, it is my prayer that if you have not been filled with the Holy Spirit, you will 'cry' out to the Lord, who is more than able and willing to fill you right here, right now. *Luke 9:13 says, "If ye then, being evil, know how to give good gifts unto your children; how much more shall your heavenly Father give the Holy Spirit to them that ask Him?* Ask Him to fill you with His Holy Spirit, with the evidence of speaking in Holy tongues, and I promise, you too will never be the same again. Stop right now and pray this simple prayer:

"Father, in the name of Jesus, I ask you to fill me with the Holy Spirit, with the evidence of speaking in other tongues as the Spirit of the Lord gives utterance. I believe by faith that it is done in Jesus' name. Amen."

I dare not end this chapter without letting you know that, being filled with the Holy Spirit has proven to be one of the most important assets of my life, as I have sought to fulfill all of God's callings. I would be remiss if I did not remind you that the call to preach is but one of several 'calls' that God gives. For certain, it is His process. Even though the gifts and callings of God are without repentance, *(Romans 11:29)* we cannot respond to one and neglect the others.

ANSWER EVERY CALL

- God calls us first unto salvation through repentance. *(Acts 2:38) "Then Peter said unto them, Repent, and be baptized every one of you in the name of Jesus Christ for the remission of sins, and ye shall receive the gift of the Holy Ghost."*
- He calls us to live a Holy life. *(I Peter 1:13-16) Wherefore gird up the loins of your mind, be sober, and hope to the end for the grace that is to be brought unto you at the revelation of Jesus Christ; As obedient children, not*

fashioning yourselves according to the former lusts in your ignorance: But as He which hath called you is holy, so be ye holy in all manner of conversation; Because it is written, Be ye holy; for I am holy.

- He calls us unto a lifelong season of study and preparation. *(II Timothy 2:15) "Study to shew thyself approved unto God, a workman that needeth not to be ashamed, rightly dividing the word of truth."*
- He calls us to release or send us forth to preach and teach. *(Matthew 28:19-20) Go ye therefore, and teach all nations, baptizing them in the name of the Father, and of the Son, and of the Holy Ghost: Teaching them to observe all things whatsoever I have commanded you: and, lo, I am with you alway, even unto the end of the world. Amen.*

It is very important to recognize which "call" you are responding to, so that you do not get ahead of God's timing. Make sure you have heard and heeded the first three calls, before you try to go forth into the preaching and teaching ministry. This will ensure your effectiveness in this life, and your reward in the life to come.

THUS LEARN:

- As a preacher you must 'know' in your heart of hearts that you are called of God.
- A human witness may encourage you, but if no man bears witness, the Holy Spirit and the Word of God must bear witness with your spirit.
- Remember that we make plans, but God's purposes prevail.
- Pray for God to open the doors of opportunity, to provide the message, and to guard His message.
- The infilling of the Holy Spirit is a priceless asset and glorious experience. Enjoy Him daily.
- An intimate relationship with God helps prepare a preacher as an effective spokesperson for Him.
- Yield to God's Spirit and receive all that He gives.
- Answer every call of God for your life.

CHAPTER 2

TALK TO YOUR PASTOR

In spite of the fact that I had finally accepted my call to preach at the age of twenty-seven, and had even been filled with the Holy Ghost, I am so glad the Lord taught me the following lesson right away. Why? Because it has proven to be one of the best of all lessons I've ever learned.

The mistake many young preachers make is trying to go it alone, or trying to rush into preaching before being prepared and released. I have heard it said, "Tis better to be a preacher who has been 'sent', instead of one who just 'went'. I believe this to be true, because some of the preachers I knew who 'went', became isolated and eventually quit. Many started out on fire, but eventually cooled off and faded from view. Because our God is a God of order, it makes sense that He would provide guidance and coverage for us through a natural spiritual leader in the earth, as well as provide guidance through His Holy Spirit. Jesus waited to hear His Father's voice of release from Heaven. He also waited for John the Baptist's voice of introduction before starting His earthly ministry. *(Matthew Chapter 3).* So, too, God told me to wait for my pastor's voice of release before starting the ministry He had given to me. I didn't completely understand why at the time, but I obeyed God and sought an appointment with my pastor to talk about this thing called 'preaching'.

At first it took a while to see him, because he was a very busy man. Nevertheless, I prayerfully and persistently pursued a place on his calendar. His secretary became very familiar with my voice, and eventually my persistence paid off. Finally, the day of the big meeting had come.

On that day, I sat nervously in the chair opposite his desk and told him I sincerely believed God had called me to preach. I never shall forget his response. After a long period of silence, he raised his eyebrows and said "well Rita, just keep on doing what you're doing and let's talk again in about a year". 'A year?' 'A year?' I was stunned. I was hurt. I was angry. I was confused. Why did I have to wait a year? It had already taken me months to get this meeting with him. Now he wanted me to wait another year? Didn't he know that I was faithfully teaching Sunday school? Didn't he know that I was already getting invitations to speak at special church services? I didn't understand. Two other young men had announced their calling, and within a couple of months pastor had allowed them to stand in front of the church and preach their "initial sermon". What was going on? Now, I knew that I was the first young woman to come forth, but why should that matter? Why?

Well, beloved, in that moment I came to the stark realization that as unfair as it was, I was facing in 1977, an age-old prejudice regarding "women in ministry". As I sat listening to my pastor talk, I found out quickly that it was acceptable for a woman to teach, or speak in Sunday school, or share in the Baptist training union, or serve on the missionary board, or speak for a women's day program— but to allow a woman to "preach" with a recognized license, was a struggle for many pastors and pew members both, male and female.

Likewise, while sitting there I began to recall that, for almost all of the pastors I knew, ordination of women was absolutely out of the question. Thus, I believe my pastor, in his struggle said, "after a year, let's talk again." Of course, his additional comment really put the icing on the cake when he said, "I may license you, but I will never ordain you". Those were his final words, and the meeting was over. In spite of the fact that it was a painfully disappointing answer, I submitted to him. I prayed and praised the pain away.

In fact, in my time of prayer, God showed me that He was building patience into me, and courage into my pastor. So, I went on working faithfully and waited for a year. I didn't leave the church, and I didn't let go of what God had revealed to me. I kept on doing the work of the Lord and serving in the local church where He had placed me. I also kept on delivering my 'speeches' as God provided opportunity.

After almost a year more of studying, teaching, singing, speaking, and serving wherever needed, my pastor called me in to see him again. This time he requested the meeting! Amazingly, this time I was not nervous. This time, as I sat across from him, he confessed that he had watched me for the year, and had seen my good works in our church and other churches as well. He admitted that he believed God's hand was upon me to preach. As a result, he gave me his blessings and released me to preach in our church.

Even though he did not have to confront the question of ordination before his death, he courageously kept his word and gave me the opportunity to preach my first 'official' sermon on March 15, 1978. He licensed me soon thereafter. It did not make him popular with men, but God used him to give me my official release into 'ministry', and the ecumenical community.

THUS LEARN:

- It is important to talk with your pastor, or his/her designated appointee if you believe you are called to preach, even if you are not sure.
- Be patient but persistent in pursuing your meeting with the pastor.
- No matter how painful it may be, submit to your pastor's decision.
- Remember, the prejudice of men does not override the purpose of God.
- Stay planted where God has put you, and bloom where you are planted.
- Know that your promotion comes from the Lord.
- The heart of your pastor is in the hand of the Lord, so pray.
- Trust God, because your times and seasons are also in His Hands.
- Know that God will allow you to be released in His time.
- Study to be ready when your time of release comes.

CHAPTER 3

MY INITIAL SERMON

I never shall forget my first `official' sermon. Back then they called it your `initial sermon' or `trial sermon'. It was the one that everyone would mark as your legitimate starting point. All of my friends, family, loved ones, well wishers, skeptics, and even a few enemies would be there to witness this momentous event. It was supposed to be an exciting experience, as `my first official time out'. However, since I had spoken in public many times before, I felt like this time would be no different. I thought it would be business as usual. Boy, was I wrong!

By the time Sunday night arrived on March 15, 1978, I was a nervous wreck. Why? Because I felt like everyone was expecting so much. I expected so much. I had dreamed of this time. I had waited patiently a whole year for this opportunity. I had written over 19 pages to preach, on lined notebook paper. I was nervous, but I honestly believed I was ready.

Unfortunately, no one had spent any time in helping me to 'get ready' for what I was about to do. There had been no lessons on sermon preparation. There had been no practice sessions. The only thing my pastor had done was to set a date and announce it to the church. We had no other meetings prior to the initial sermon.

No one offered me the advice a young preacher needs prior to the initial sermon. Not my pastor or another pastor I admired. I had visited his Bible study class from time to time, and had cornered him often, to ask questions about the scriptures which were exploding inside me. I enjoyed our exchanges, and gleaned much, as he shared marvelous insights into the Word of God. In many ways I viewed him as my mentor, since, I had discussed my calling with him. However, he never offered any advice or instruction to me concerning 'preaching', or sermon preparation.

Consequently, because I didn't know what to ask, and no one took me aside to school me, let me tell you that the night of my initial sermon proved to be the worst preaching nightmare I have ever experienced —and I mean ever!

On that night the church was filled with people. Mom, dad, all my brothers and sisters, the Mt. Pleasant Baptist

Church family, many other church members, co-workers and good friends were present. All of the people I had invited—and more were there, but I didn't really see them. The choir sang all the right songs to set the atmosphere for good preaching, but I didn't hear a sound. I sat in the preacher's coveted center seat, but I didn't feel it under me. I was surrounded by plenty of preachers and deacons, sitting in swivel chairs, offering sincere 'Amens', but I never heard a word!

From the time my pastor introduced me and I stood up, to the moment I finally sat down again, all I remember is that I was so petrified I could hardly breathe. There was not one relaxed bone in my body. My hands were glued to the podium. My eyes were riveted to, and never left, the nineteen pages of notes I had written. My personality was nowhere to be found, and nothing, absolutely nothing but the merciful compassion and grace of God got all of us through the agony of that hour.

I remember that I started in the book of Genesis and ended in the book of Revelation, even though my text was *Romans 6:23.* I don't even remember the subject, the introduction, or any particular points. And, as far as the conclusion and the ending were concerned, I just remember reading the last line of page 19 and feeling so humiliated, that the gracious claps I heard when I sat down were no consolation at all.

As I sat I just knew I had blown it forever. This thought was further cemented in my spirit, when my own pastor got up and said that although I had "milked a good bucket of milk, I had kicked it over". His words were kind enough and completely accurate, but still had a devastating effect on my spirit. In addition, the pastor I so admired was overheard to say that although I was a great teacher, the thought of me preaching was a 'Joke'. Words cannot express the heartbreak I felt. I admired him so, and thought he believed in me. Needless to say, one of many hard lessons I learned that night, was that you should never put your trust in men for affirmation. Your expectation should be of God and God alone.

Years later, by the grace of God, before these two pastors went to be with the Lord, they both changed their minds about my preaching. To God Be the Glory! Interestingly, in the beginning, God used them and their words to provoke me to become the preacher He wanted me to be. I learned more through failure (in my mind) than through success. I realized the necessity of learning the art (homiletics), and science (hermeneutics) of preaching.

THUS LEARN:

- Do not go on your own as a beginner. Please wait to be released into ministry.
- As a minister who is just starting, do not assume you know anything about preaching.
- Pursue your pastor for guidance in preparing to preach. If classes are available, welcome them.
- Ask questions about everything when you are not sure. The only bad question is the question you do not ask.
- Following your pastor's guidance, prepare an outline from your study notes.
- Review your message with your pastor.
- Practice preaching your message from the outline, to yourself in the mirror, to your pastor, and others, if they will listen.
- Practice will help relax you and allow you to be yourself.
- Be yourself! And don't forget to breathe.
- Know that ultimately God is the only one you have to please, but do work to please Him.
- Take criticisms, counsel, and compliments alike to the Lord.
- Let God's voice be the final voice you hear, and obey.

CHAPTER 4

GOOD PREACHING AND GOOD FELLOWSHIP

For weeks after my initial sermon I remember wanting to hide, but the invitations kept on coming. In the first year, I recall getting one invitation each month. That may not seem like many, but as a beginner it took me the whole month to prepare one message. I would study, write, pray, and fast in order to 'Hear from God'. He very graciously answered my original prayer to Him and gave me somewhere and something to preach. He also used others to train me in the art of preaching.

I remember driving for hours to hear good preachers, in order to glean whatever I could from them. I attended the Hampton Ministers Conference (when women were hardly being recognized as preachers), just to hear some of God's finest preachers, because I loved good preaching! In truth, thoughts of my own personal inadequacy prompted me to constantly seek good preaching. I didn't care who was doing it as long as it was good. I listened to men like the renowned Billy Graham, D.E. King, Manuel Scott, Sr., James Forbes, Jr., Gardner Taylor, Howard Thurmond, A.L. Patterson, W.A. Jones, and lesser known but just as anointed preachers, such as Anthony Wilcox, Jasper Rolle, Kenneth Moales, Freddie Davis, Alfred and Susie Owens, David Durham, Robert Williams, and yes, T.D. Jakes. I went wherever I had to go in order to hear good preaching.

I heard good preaching and I talked good preaching. Whenever I got a chance to talk with my peers, we didn't talk about the weather, the economy or politics. Just as doctors talk about good medicine, or golfers talk about good golfing, as preachers we talked about good preaching. We talked about the text; we talked about style; we talked about content. How did they open? What were the story lines? How did they tie up the message? What about the close? You know, good preaching. Did they "hoop" or did they sing? These were points that we wanted to know.

When I came along in 1978, there were other young ministers I knew who were also just getting started. We were about twenty-five in number, and many of us were having similar experiences of rejection, or acceptance with limitations, from pastors and pew members alike. Preaching was everything to us as young ministers of the gospel. Thankfully, one brave young pastor named Robert Williams took us under his wings. He taught us ministry basics and loaned us his church so we could practice preaching to each other on Saturday mornings. We became a fellowship of ministers, (male and female) who supported each other without prejudice. Whenever one of us had an invitation to preach, all of us would get together and go in support. Pastors and churches were amazed at the fellowship we shared. One for all, and all for one! Many times, as a fellowship of ministers, we made up the majority of the congregation.

On Saturdays, preaching to my brothers and sisters who were rookies just like me was exciting, and yet painful. I say exciting, because they (my fellow rookie preachers) were a loyal congregation that would not walk out on you. Also, as a fellowship group we always gave an offering to the preacher of the morning. Everyone got a turn to preach, so everyone got an offering. In addition, since there were only about twenty-five of us, we all got to preach to the group on two Saturday mornings. Funny thing is that for some of us, those two offerings were the best offerings we received all year!

I said exciting, and yet painful. Why painful? Because those same preacher brothers and sisters who stayed and gave offerings would also critique the message and messenger without mercy. Sound doctrine, correct homiletics, proper attire, diction, eye contact, time —you name it, we evaluated it. The Lord knows they stayed on me about being long-winded, even though they applauded the messages I preached.

Believe it or not, for some of us, after these years, we still send offerings to each other and critique each other. We are still there for each other at a moment's call. Today, they don't say I preach long any more, because many of them preach as long as I do, or longer. And yet, all of those who are pastors still send for me to come and preach to their congregations. I go, fully expecting a good offering and an honest critique. I would not have it any other way, and I have not been disappointed.

As iron sharpens iron, good preachers should sharpen and provoke each other unto excellence in preaching. It has been said that practice makes perfect. I believe perfection is a moving target, and being perfected is an ongoing process. Suffice it to say that 'practice' is a significant part of the process, and as such, really does help one become better and better. I can say this, because out of our 'practicing' fellowship, God has called Pastors, Evangelists, Prophets, Teachers and Apostles who are operating very effectively in the Kingdom today. Praise God!

Another benefit has been the life long friendships that have come from this fellowship of ministers. As a result, ministry networks have been created throughout the country. We can call upon each other today, and help will be on the way. I thank God for all of the ministers I have shared fellowship with down through the years, and for new 'fellows' that He is adding to the 'ship' even now. Also, I am grateful that the Lord taught me early to appreciate diversity in fellowship, because all of us can help each other.

As for the original ministerial fellowship, today we are all very busy in ministry, and cannot get together as often as we would like. However, when we do get together, in spite of all we have been through, and even with all we have accomplished, the thing we still enjoy talking about most is the thing we just can't seem to get enough of 'good preaching'! The heart and soul of our conversation as preachers is still: how to rightly divide the word we preach; how to improve on the way we preach; how to be the very best preacher we can be; how to win more souls with our preaching; and, what it is going to be like when Jesus comes back and rewards us for preaching. In other words, we are obsessed with 'good preaching', and being 'good preachers'. I believe this is a 'good thing'!

THUS LEARN:

- God's calling on your life is not dependent upon you, your feelings, or the feelings of others.
- God will not hand you more than you can handle.
- Do your very best with every God-Given opportunity.
- Be the best you can be, for Jesus will be rewarding each of us.
- No matter how hot it is, a lump of coal will cool off quickly if it is left alone.
- Always get everything you can get, from good preaching.
- Pursue fellowship with good preachers.
- Be willing to give and receive support as a preacher.
- Know that good fellowship can result in lifelong friendships.
- Never forget that 'fellows' in the 'ship' need each other for the trip.

CHAPTER 5

PAYING DUES

ANSWERED PRAYER

Since I received confirmation from the Lord, I always embraced my call to preach. Nevertheless, as a maturing preacher, I realized that there were dues I had to pay. I felt a strong urgency to 'get it right'. I wanted to be an answer to prayer. I wanted to be a preacher that would bring God Glory. So, I prayed again the prayer I mentioned earlier, with even greater sincerity.

> *"Lord, please give me somewhere to preach, something to preach, and don't let me preach error."*

This time, my reason for asking God's favor in this three-fold prayer, was being motivated by what I had been observing among preachers. There were some preachers who would call pastors and solicit an invitation to preach. I did not want to do that, because I believed God would open doors for me.

I knew of other preachers who stood to preach, but were obviously not prepared with a message. They rambled on and on, often groping for words to fill in the time. I did not want to do that either, because I believed that a preacher should be prepared.

There were times I listened intently for scripture while a preacher was speaking, only to discover that some preachers were not given to the study of God's Word. As a result, they would misquote, misinterpret, or in some cases simply misuse the scriptures to support their own personal bias. For sure, I never wanted to be guilty of preaching my own prejudices or biases. I just wanted to preach Jesus Christ. Thus, this three-fold prayer became my heart's cry even the more!

> *"Lord, please give me somewhere to preach, something to preach and don't let me preach error."*

God answered my prayer completely. How? First, from the day of my initial sermon until now, I have never had to ask anyone for an opportunity to preach. The Lord has opened wide the door for me to preach and teach the gospel of Jesus Christ. All of my engagement invitations have resulted from 'word of mouth' communications among pastors and church members. Although I started out primarily in the Baptist community of churches (Primitive, Progressive, Fundamental, Institutional, Missionary, Southern, National, Full Gospel), the Lord allowed my gift to make room for me in many other Christian communities. I began to receive invitations from the Methodist circle of churches (United, African Methodist Episcopal, African Methodist Episcopal Zion and Christian Methodist Episcopal).

Then, He allowed me to receive invitations from the Lutheran, Presbyterian, Catholic, Seventh Day Adventist, Assembly of God, Church of God, Church of God in Christ, Pentecostal Assemblies of the World, Bible Way Worldwide, Old fashioned Holiness, Native American Indian and other non-denominational churches too numerous to name. Whether the congregation was black, white, red, yellow, brown, or mixed, every opportunity afforded me a unique experience with God and His people, and I thank God to this day for His GREAT favor!

In all of these arenas, I have found that people are essentially the same, and that they have the same basic needs. I also quickly discovered that the simple Gospel of Jesus Christ would meet the needs of God's people and win lost souls, no matter where they were. Why? The simple truth is we all need peace, and joy, and love, and salvation. In other words, we all need Jesus!

Therefore, since God called me to give them Jesus, He took complete responsibility for providing somewhere for me to preach. Then He assured me that although He is unimpressed by my natural ability, He would equip me with His supernatural ability, based upon my availability to Him. The reality is that God will provide both the place and the message for the preacher, if we will truly make ourselves available to Him.

My friend Jeffrey Reed once told me, "Rita, no one lays down a blunder and wakes up a wonder. There are no over-night successes. So, learn to be patient with yourself and with God. Stay available to Him, and trust Him to open the doors that will allow your gift to make room for you." I did my part. God did His part. Beloved, Jeffrey was right!

Young, inexperienced preachers, who may be full of zeal, don't have the necessary amount of wisdom and knowledge right away. It takes time to add knowledge to zeal. It takes time and experience to attain wisdom, which is the application of knowledge. What I am really saying is that there are no shortcuts to gaining anything. Time given to consistent study adds knowledge. Living, learning, and applying life's lessons each day, adds wisdom. In addition, God will give us wisdom if we ask Him, but He gives it in His own time and way. The development of one's own unique style in ministry takes time. Knowing how to respond to certain situations, tests, or trials takes time. Maturing into a balanced effective ministry gift takes time. Any preacher, who is willing to invest the time, will eventually be noted as a `wonder', and not a `blunder'. Learning this truth was a very important part of God's plan as He opened doors for me.

Also, I believe God sent me to places where some other ministers would not go. Through this process, He proved my faithfulness to Him, and His faithfulness to me. For example, some preachers would only take engagements in churches that had a large membership and guaranteed them a certain amount in their offering. This didn't seem like `an offering' to me, if there was already a required amount stipulated. But that was just my opinion. Often, God sent me to churches that had only a handful of people. Of course, He would show up, bless us spiritually, and bless me financially through the offering in spite of the numbers.

Then, God sent me to some churches that were just getting started. My assignment was to encourage the pastor. Whenever I felt led by the Holy Spirit, I would even return the offering to the church. It's funny how some preachers thought I was crazy for sowing offerings back into ministries. All I know is that as I went and obeyed Him faithfully, God made me an answer to many prayers, and absolutely proved His faithfulness to me!

In some instances the Lord used me to bring order and instruction to beginning ministries, with the pastor's permission, of course. There were even times the Lord sent me to a church, with a confirming word of prophecy, at the time the church needed that Word the most. My heart and spiritual ear were available to God, and my commitment was to speak whatever He said. As He sharpened my ear, He blessed me as well as His people.

I thank God that He wouldn't let me be a preacher who only went to already established churches. I went over the river and through the woods, wherever the Lord sent me, with a heart full of gratitude and faith, and a Word from Him. Hallelujah!

One of the things I would caution preachers to avoid is, wanting to sit in 'big' pulpits. The preacher who pushes his or her own agenda, trying to make a 'big' name for him or herself, has already missed the objective of true ministry —which is to be a servant of the people for Christ. The main challenge of any preacher is to avoid becoming egotistical once the 'gift' of God does make room, and the accolades begin to follow. We must be careful dear preacher, lest we forget Calvary!

The other area of caution is to become satisfied with what happened yesterday. You know, the way the Holy Ghost showed up and showed off. The way the altar filled to capacity. The way the Voice of God came roaring through while you preached. Wonderful! Praise The Lord! But don't stop. As preachers, we do not have a 'spiritual parking zone'. We cannot allow yesterday's victories to hinder tomorrow's work.

At times I have wanted to be satisfied with yesterday's accomplishments, but the people who really loved me wouldn't allow me to become complacent and lazy. When I think of those who have pushed me towards excellence in ministry, Pat and Terry Streeter come to mind. Many days, one of them would call and ask how the ministry was going. Then in their own way, each of them would challenge me to push out all they believed was in me. Pat used to say, "girly girl, you provoke so many of these men to do better. And, you encourage the women to get going. Don't stop now. Keep inspiring them all to be the best they can be, by being the very best preacher you can be". That really encouraged me. On the other hand, Terry claims that he taught me all I know. Well, I do know for certain that he has always provoked me to keep on learning.

Of course, there are many other preachers who have inspired me to seek continued excellence in ministry, by being tremendous examples themselves. Bishop Ralph Dennis is a stellar example of integrity as an Apostolic Father, and preacher of God's Word. My sister in the ministry, Pastor Jackie McCullough, is a wonderful example of one who is committed to rightly dividing the Word of Truth. Bishop Ernestine C. Reems-Dickerson is a pioneer of women in ministry, that leads the way by the light of her life and her life's work. Bishop Joseph Garlington, the consummate worship leader, reminds me never to forget my first love. Bishop Arthur Brazier shows me that I can age gracefully while powerfully preaching the gospel. Of course, Bishop T.D. Jakes, Sr., as father, coach, pastor, and mentor does not allow me any space or time to be 'at ease in Zion'. His drive in pursuit of excellence has irrevocably infected my life. His relentless pace challenges me to go and do, even when I would rather sit and daydream. Likewise, many other precious brothers and sisters push me in many ways to reach my full potential. Day by day, I see my potential being unlocked, as I am constantly motivated by many to 'Press toward the mark for the prize of the High calling of God in Christ Jesus'. *(Philippians 3:14)*

Whenever I become discouraged and want to quit (I am human), my best friend Frances is right there to lift my spirit by saying, "Rita, don't faint now. Remember that the real payday will not happen down here!"

I thank God for everyone in my life that wants me to be all I can be for the Lord. Most of all I thank Him, because He wants me to be all I can be —and He encourages me the most! Likewise, may I encourage you also, to be all you absolutely can be in service to our King. If you do, I can assure you that God will make you an answer to someone's prayer.

Finally, if ever I am tempted to show off the gift God has given me, the Holy Spirit whispers in my ear. He tells me to remember that it is still God's Kingdom, God's power, and above all God's Glory! So, I can't help but continue to pursue excellence and give God all the praise. The Lord has opened many doors, and allowed me to preach the gospel continuously for over twenty-five years. In this area, He has blessed me tremendously. I do not take His favor for granted. God does answer prayer!

SOMETHING TO PREACH

Secondly, for every opportunity God has sent my way, He has given me a message from His heart for His people. As I have been faithful to study and seek His heart, He has faithfully given me revelation and illumination of His Word. I would not think of trying to speak for or about Him, without first hearing His voice!

That wise pastor I mentioned earlier named David Durham once told me, "Rita, stay in the Word of God, because it is the safest place in the whole wide world for a preacher. Do not preach your doubts, because people have enough doubts of their own. Preach only out of your heart's conviction and understanding of God's Word, not just what you have heard; and, preach the whole counsel of God! Like the mailman delivers the mail, deliver the Word, no matter when, where, or under what circumstance. If God has provided the opportunity to do so, deliver the mail, daughter— Preach the Word! And live the message you preach, in spite of how hard it might be." Amen, Pastor David. I thank God that, because I took pastor David's advice, and have kept studying, over the years God has answered part number two of my prayer. I have not had to grope for words, or buy a message, or imitate anyone else as I preach. Nor have I hesitated to preach whatever God has given, even in times of personal trials. In so doing, I have been sanctified and sustained by the same Word I have preached to others!

DON'T PREACH ERROR

Finally, to my knowledge, I have not preached 'error'. By this I mean doctrinal, theological, or thematic error. Sure I have made mistakes from time to time in names or dates and the like, but I have not ever felt the need to apologize for the content of any message I have preached. I have purposed to stay at Jesus' feet and glean the 'good part', which is intimacy with Him. This has led to a greater accuracy in the delivery of His Word. I know I have to keep growing, so I continue to study and pray for understanding, that I might be a workman who is well able to rightly divide the Word of Truth. And today, in these three areas, I give God all glory and praise for answered prayer!

I OWE, I OWE

Now, please understand that with answered prayer there are dues to pay. The one thing I learned quickly about prayer is that you should never pray a prayer if you are not willing to be a part of its answer. God loves to 'labor together' with us in building His Kingdom. He is a Father who includes His children in the family business (soul winning); and if we are willing, He will win many souls through us. He will use us to lay hands on the sick as we pray and He will heal them. He will use us to take food to the hungry, and not just pray for them. He will use us to visit the prison bound that we have been asking Him to bless. God intends to deliver, but like with Moses and the children of Israel, He intends to use us as instruments of deliverance in His Hand. So, don't even think that you will get away with just asking

God to bless, when in fact you may have the blessing your hand, or may be the blessing in His Hand.

In accordance with this truth, God gave me all I asked, and then required that I prove faithful to what I had requested. In other words, I had to be willing to go and fulfill each invitation accepted, even if I didn't feel like it physically or emotionally. In such cases, I just had to go through, and go on. No matter where, with or without support, whatever the size of the congregation, God expected me to preach the message He gave me to the best of my ability every time I stood. This meant that I had to study constantly, and remain available to the Lord for fresh revelation and increased knowledge of His Word.

As I showed myself willing and faithful to prepare and deliver, He showed Himself faithful to provide opportunities, send messages, and guard His truth as it proceeded out of my mouth. I lovingly adopted the following motto: "I owe, I owe, so off to work I go." **I had to pay my dues!**

Even though I prayed 'Lord unless you do it, it won't be done'; and even though I was completely depending on Him; I still had to pay my dues! So, I would go. By plane, train, or automobile I would go. Mile after mile, day after day, city after city, I would go to preach. Whether in a cathedral, or a store front, or an office suite, or a house living room, or a school auditorium, or on a street corner, or under a tent, or in a senior citizens home, or in a prison yard, or in a back yard, or in a park, or from the back of a parked truck; no matter where, I would go at least once to preach or minister. (I will talk more a bit later about the concept of going anywhere at least once to preach or minister.)

During the first ten years of preaching, from 1978 to 1988 —I call them "the early years", I would go without hesitancy, help, and, unfortunately, sometimes without regard for my health. (Allow me to also address this matter of health in greater detail later.)

Beloved, I studied. I traveled. I preached. I would go home to sleep. Then, once awake again, I would study, travel and preach. Of course the frequency had increased to better than once a week instead of once a month. Though preaching more, I still listened to good preachers. I had no personal preacher mentor in the beginning, but I can truly tell you that over the years, just 'paying dues' has helped to school me in many ways. While going forth to do my best, I constantly listened to preachers. Young and old, any color, and any culture; I always expected to learn something of ministry from each one. As a result, fresh revelation, insightful interpretation, and constant inspiration were the priceless rewards for my seeking!

THUS LEARN:

- God has the message. It is our responsibility to seek Him, and prepare ourselves as the messenger.
- People do not care how much you know until they know how much you care; so let the love of God shine through wherever you go.
- God taught me personally that if I put a price on preaching, I would be putting a limit on Him. However, if I would trust Him to provide, He would be an unlimited source of abundant supply.
- Stay under pastoral covering and remain faithful to work in your local church, even as you go out to preach.
- Love God, love His Word, love His people, love His work, and you will always have job security in His Kingdom.

CHAPTER 6

PROTOCOL

HONOR

Having been brought up as a military child, I learned something very important through observation. My dad was an officer in the Air Force. As such, many times I saw men and women salute him as they passed. He would quickly return their salute. I felt so proud to be walking with him, so one day I asked him why they had saluted. He told me that it was his rank that had earned their salute. Not his color, or his gender, but his rank. In addition, I saw my dad salute other officers whose rank was higher than his, never thinking it demeaning to do so. He knew they deserved his salute as well. In that natural setting I soon realized that honor came with rank or position, and that promotion to a higher rank or position came as a result of the person being skilled, and of course, `paying their dues'. Years of service and skill had earned my dad and many others the right to be honored and saluted. Through this observation, I learned that protocol was important. What is protocol? The definition that makes sense to me is this: ceremonial forms, customs, and courtesies, which are accepted as proper and correct in a particular setting or situation.

As I studied the subject of protocol more, I found that this is also a Biblical principle. In *Romans 13:7*, Paul commands us to *"Render therefore to all their dues: tribute to whom tribute is due; custom to whom custom; fear to whom fear; honor to whom honor."* This makes reference to those in spiritual authority over us, as well as those in the natural, whose `dues' have earned them the rank and right to be, as it were, `saluted' with honor. Some examples might include the honor we give policemen, judges, the president, and many others based upon their positions. In addition, it includes obeying the laws of the land, giving an honest day's work for an honest day's pay, paying taxes or child support... I think you get my point.

Therefore, to apply this principle in ministry, every time I went to another preacher's house (church), I would salute and give honor: first, to God (whose house it really was); to the pastor (who had been given stewardship over the house); to the spouse and family of the pastor; to the ranking leadership; and, to the general membership. Here is an example of what might be appropriate:

> First giving honor to God; to Pastor Billy Best; to his lovely first lady Mrs. Bertha Best and the first family; to the clergy, deacons, officers, mothers, saints and friends of *The Way Of The Cross Church.* I thank God for the privilege of being here today to share the precious 'bread of life'... *(these names are fictitious).*

In those first few moments of saluting and honoring the people whose position, rank, service, and experience had earned them the right to receive it, I too received something special. God would place those I honored into my hands, and give me their full attention and support. In other words, as I paid attention to this aspect of 'protocol', The Lord called their hearts and minds to 'attention', so that they might willingly hear what He had given me to say.

I am so glad He taught me this lesson, because it paved the way into the hearts of many pastors and congregations. They sensed right away that I respected them and their people. In response, most would lean forward and offer verbal as well as non-verbal assent to what I was saying. In turn, congregations would be challenged to follow the example of their leaders. Believe me when I say that it is very important to have the support and favorable attention of the pastor. Thus, effective use of protocol is a major key to success in this aspect of ministry.

Protocol has worked for me in churches of all denominations, sizes, cultures, races and creeds. Why? Because people want to be, and honestly do have the right to be 'saluted', for the time they have given in the service of the Lord. Ministry means sacrifices. Servants of The Lord, true servants, make personal sacrifices, along with their families. So, to take a moment and honor what they have contributed is not robbery. No one wants to be overlooked or slighted. The simple acknowledgement of those who have helped to build and serve the ministry, creates an attitude of good will that is most valuable. Because I have taken the time to honor pastors and their congregations, they have returned the honor by listening to me, and in many instances by inviting me back. My desire has been to always leave the house of God better off than when I came. Honor and respect for God's people is a part of that process.

HEAVENLY PROTOCOL

Giving glory and honor to God is always appropriate. It takes precedence over everything else. In fact, the highest form of protocol is honoring God! All I have to do is think of His Goodness. I cannot begin to articulate the love and gratitude I feel every single day of my life for the love and favor God has shown me.

I know some may think that favor is a small thing, but for me it is a clear indication of God's unfailing love. As much as I travel, favor is receiving an unexpected upgrade to business or first class. Favor is having a plane that should have already taken off, still waiting at the gate, when I am frantically running late. Favor is giving the last seat on an overbooked flight to me, even though I am only on stand-by status. Favor is finding a parking space up front in a crowded parking lot, so that I can make a flight, in spite of the fact that I have over slept. These are just a few of the ways I see God's hand of favor readily working in my daily life. When these kinds of things happen, I usually stop for a moment of what I call heavenly protocol. I shout. I whisper "thank you". I shed a tear of joy, and send up sincere praise, as I recall again the awesome truth that my God favors me.

Favor, however, goes far beyond matters related to just travel. God's favor touches every aspect of my life. In fact, just being able to preach for Him is an expression of His great favor toward me. He is always looking out for, making a way for, and opening doors for me! Through the preaching of the gospel, my life is constantly transformed. Certainly, the message He gives me to give to others, reminds me constantly of His great love and care for us all. I can't help but reverence, and honor such an awesome, sovereign God. Nothing in this world can compare with the love and favor I receive from my God! Hallelujah! So for me, taking a moment anytime, anywhere, for any reason, to acknowledge and give God the glory, and honor, and praise, is always appropriate and in order. Again, I call it 'Heavenly Protocol'!

UNDERSTANDING

There is another element of protocol I must share, which deals with being governed in any pastor's church. My mother taught me as a child to respect the rules and property in another person's home. Likewise, the Lord taught me to respect another preacher's pulpit. This is how. First, God told me to always communicate with the pastor before going to teach or preach. This time of communication would allow me to hear the pastor's heart and vision for the house, plus any expectation he or she might have.

Getting an understanding of expectations is very important. For, one real meaning of '**understanding**' is '**standing under**', or being submitted to the pastor whose house you are going to serve. Please believe me when I tell you that, knowing and honoring what is expected of you, is just as important as giving honor with your lips. This includes knowing the customs and beliefs of the pastor, knowing the order and timing of the service, and being governed by the instructions given to you.

I thank God that through communication with the pastors, and by listening earnestly to Him, I have never knowingly offended any pastor, or preached anything that would contradict or be in conflict with what was being taught in any particular church. Even if I knew of differences in our beliefs, God taught me never to disrespect or speak in contradiction to a pastor in his or her pulpit. We might have enlightening discussions after service in the study, but in the pulpit there always had to be agreement. And since my assignment was simply to preach the Gospel of Jesus Christ, because I did just that, I had 'no problems,' and to my knowledge, did not create any.

LEAVE IT BETTER

Next, God taught me that protocol has everything to do with leaving a house in better condition than you found it. So, as I traveled from church to church, I soon learned the importance of being a blessing wherever I went. I believed *Acts 20:35* which says it is more blessed to give than to receive. I believed Matthew 10:8 which teaches freely ye have received, freely give. I also believed my grandmother who taught me that you can't beat God giving, and only what you do for Christ will last. With all these truths in my spirit, I would head out to each church for the express purpose of being a blessing, and leaving the people of God 'better off' because of my coming.

Certainly, there were times when I was not appreciated or taken care of by some pastors and churches. However, God, who was pleased with my heart's intent and effort, would use someone else to make up for what another man did not do. At times, I was disappointed in certain pastors. At times, I was angry. At times, I cried, but I always had the peace of knowing that I had done my best as unto the Lord, and that He would supply all my need.

> *"And whatsoever ye do, do it heartily, as to the Lord, and not unto men; Knowing, that of the Lord ye shall receive the reward of the inheritance: for ye serve the Lord Christ." Colossians 3:23-24*

As I grew in grace, His pleasure became my ultimate reward. Money, or the lack of it, and man's appreciation, or the lack of it, could not compare to the joy and peace that was mine at the end of the day. So, observing proper protocol was not a burden. It was mine to give as unto the Lord, and the reward was mine to receive at the hand of the Lord!

TAKE CARE OF THE HANDS

I find that one of the most important aspects of protocol is hardly ever discussed. My grandmother told me something one day as a little girl that I have never forgotten: "Rita, always say thank you, and show your appreciation. Why? Because people don't have to be nice, and if they are nice, they don't have to be nice to you!" I filed her sayings under "First Grandmother Chapter 1". I made myself a promise to always show people the appreciation that I would want to receive, for kindness shown or service given. I call it taking care of the hands that take care of you!

As a traveling preacher, this principle of kindness translated into words of gratitude and generous tips for everyone who helped or served me. I tipped the skycap or redcap who checked my bags, the doorman and the bellman at the hotel, room service delivery personnel, and the housekeeping staff that cleaned my room. I also purposed to be very kind to waiters or waitresses (one of my former professions). I was so generous in fact, that as I traveled week after week, people would remember me from previous encounters, and rush to my assistance. I did not 'over' tip, because that would have been patronizing. However, I showed my appreciation consistently. Whether by airplane or train, whether in the Motel Six or in the Ritz Carlton, I have purposed to treat the people who serve me with the same kindness I would want if the tables were turned. As time has passed, I have always tried diligently to take care of the hands that take care of me. Consequently, many hands have taken very good care of me over the years, even to this present day.

Also, I've learned to always compliment a job well done by anyone who serves me, because my words of life and encouragement could keep a good servant from fainting in well doing. Sincere compliments can be the words that add new fuel and motivate a good servant to pursue an even greater level of excellence. Remember that *Hebrews 10:24* teaches us to provoke one another unto good works. All of us need to be encouraged when we do well. 'Good Job' really blesses the heart of a true servant. The bottom line is, every chance you get, strive to be a blessing.

CONFIDENTIALITY

At anytime, the preacher may be called upon to lend an ear to hear or a shoulder to cry on. When these occasions arise, it is extremely important that confidentiality be guarded. Unless the law specifically requires disclosure, a person's confidence and trust should be honored. Therefore, it is necessary that the preacher be acquainted with the legal protocol that is in place, along with any governing statutes. Ask if you do not know. Do not presume anything. Laws change constantly, and liability can only be avoided through knowledge and compliance.

VISITATIONS

In these special times, prayer and words of comfort or encouragement can be very effective. However, you should not take too long. Also, to avoid possible impropriety or misconceptions of any sort, Jesus' method should be employed for visitation of members. Remember that He sent His disciples out two by two. Take someone with you. The same applies where counseling is concerned. In this very sensitive area, much care should be given to understanding the laws that are in place, plus any education, certification, or bonding that may be required. If you are a minister, you should seek pastoral covering and instruction. If you are a senior pastor, you especially should stay abreast of the changing statutes, and pass all pertinent information on to those you cover.

WEDDINGS AND FUNERALS

As ministers, what we are able to do in each of these services may vary. For example, in some states and in many churches, the minister must be ordained and registered, in order to do the pronouncement and sign the official marriage license. Then it becomes the minister's additional responsibility to check the license before the ceremony, and mail the license in for official recordation afterwards. This information should be researched to avoid possible embarrassment.

Likewise, the official committal of the body at an interment is usually reserved for ministers who have been ordained, and granted the rite to do so by an accepted religious entity. Please consult with your pastor for training before striking out on your own.

In each of these services, very funny things are likely to happen from time to time. Such as: the groom's pants falling down, or the bride's wig coming off, or the minister's teeth popping out, or the psalmist who absolutely cannot sing. Although you may really want to just fall out laughing, please resist the temptation. Do everything humanly possible to maintain dignity and proper decorum, and God will bless you.

ORDINANCES

To be sure, the ordinances of the church must not be taken lightly. Each, in its own way exalts Jesus. Each should be given our utmost reverence and effort as we administer them to the flock of God.

Baptism – This symbolizes our identification with the death, burial, and resurrection of our Lord. If you as a minister are ever called upon to actually baptize or assist in baptism, there should first be a time of training. Pursue this important aspect of ministry with your pastor. Ask him or her to train you. Do not take for granted that you can do what you see, without learning, practicing, and mastering the techniques that are involved. It is a time of great personal intimacy and celebration for the individual. It can also be a time of great liability, if not properly handled. Be sure to give the act of baptism, and the person being baptized, the respect and honor you would want to receive if it were you. And don't forget to celebrate the new life of each candidate in Jesus' name!

Communion – This is one of the high points of our Christian experience. It is our time of personal and corporate intimacy with our Savior. This is the service we do in remembrance of Him as He has asked. We remember and appreciate His great sacrifice, with hearts of thanksgiving and praise —until He comes! Therefore, as God's minister, I implore you to give this blessed service the weight of glory it so richly deserves. Again, talk to your pastor, because it is imperative that adequate training be received before you embark upon such a high and holy service. In addition, most churches allow only ordained individuals to handle and serve the communion elements. Even if you are ordained, do not presume to serve. Wait to be invited as a participant. Be sure to understand and be governed by the protocol of each church you serve, starting with your own.

HUMILITY

As a final note on protocol, let me share an old pastor's story:

> *It seems there was a young man who was invited to preach at a large well, known church. The pastor was an older seasoned man who really wanted the young preacher to succeed, even though the young preacher was arrogant and thought more highly of himself than he should have. On the Sunday he was asked to preach, the young preacher entered the pulpit with a conceited, pompous, arrogant attitude. With head held high, and chest stuck out, he quickly proceeded to 'flunk or bomb' completely in his preaching assignment. Afterwards, in total humiliation, he prepared to exit the pulpit with his ego deflated and his head bowed down low in humility. As he was leaving the pulpit, the old seasoned pastor gave him words of wisdom (that I still hear every time I enter a pulpit). He said, "Young man, if you had gone into the pulpit the way you came out, you would have come out of the pulpit the way you went in."*

What a costly, but priceless lesson of humility for that young man to learn! I'm just glad I learned it from someone else's experience rather than my own. Now, because I have shared it with you, hopefully you will benefit from it as well. I *Peter 5:5-6* teaches that God resists the proud but gives grace to the humble. So, we should humble ourselves therefore under the mighty hand of God that He may exalt us in due time. It is the proper, and powerful thing to do.

THUS LEARN:

- Paying dues earns one the right to be honored, and there are no short cuts.
- Be quick to sow seeds of honor. They will come back to you as a mighty harvest.
- In protocol it is important to know 'who to call', so do not be afraid to ask.
- Communication with the pastor is essential to success in any church.
- Call to ensure agreement regarding customs, order and expectations.
- When in doubt, take the conservative route.
- Do not mess up another preacher's house. One day you may have your own.
- Be a blessing through protocol, and you will receive many a call.

- You don't get a second chance to make a 'first' impression.
- Take care of the hands that take care of you.
- Say 'thank you' —it lingers in the mind and waters the heart.
- Pay close attention to the details of protocol.
- Get the necessary education regarding the legal aspects of ministry.
- Humility costs you nothing. Arrogance can cost you everything.

CHAPTER 7

CHANGING THE ATMOSPHERE

I have discovered in going from church to church, conference to conference, pulpit to pulpit, and platform to platform, that in some places the people are not always ready for the release of God's Word at the time I stand to preach. In such instances, the atmosphere may need to be changed. Because of this, I must lean on the Lord to know what to do, that His Word might go forth unhindered. Establishing an anointed atmosphere, where reverence, honor, praise, and order abound, is so important. It helps prepare the people to receive the Word of God.

In this regard, I quickly began to understand, that sensitivity and obedience to the Holy Spirit is essential. First, let me say that obedience is a decision. Certainly, sensing what God wants to have happen next is something your spirit can do, only as you are open to Him personally. Remember, you cannot teach what you do not know, and you cannot lead where you do not go! I have learned that the people are like sheep that need a shepherd, to will lead them beside the still waters into the presence of the Lord. I am the shepherd of the moment. Therefore, I have to head for the still waters in the presence of the Lord myself. I must be fed, before I can feed. I must be led, before I can lead. In order to receive what I need, I must worship! This is not hard for me now, because I have been a worshipper all of my saved life. I am so grateful that the Lord showed me years ago, this 'good part' *(Luke 10:39-42)*, that is received through worship. At times, people have laughed at me as a worshipper. Yet, Jesus has never laughed at me, or taken from me, the 'good part of Him' that worship gives. Through **worship**, I receive peace, joy, patience, and direction, which enable me to handle any atmosphere I may face. In addition, I have found that as worship works for me, it will also work for others, if I lead the way.

There are many tools that can be employed in worship. For example, the **hymns** of the church have proven to be a priceless asset to me down through the years. From the first time I sang a hymn at five years of age, entitled "The Old Rugged Cross" until now, sharing my worship experience, by singing the hymns of Zion with the saints, helps to anchor my soul and theirs to Christ— no matter what the atmosphere may be.

I further believe that all of the verses of a hymn are important, because they combine to tell the whole story of the author's particular experience with the Lord. Again, my grandmother used to say, "sing all the verses Rita, because every verse builds upon the previous one, and you need to know the conclusion of the story as well as the beginning." Grandmother was right! For example, I sing all the verses of 'There is a Fountain Filled With Blood'. *William Cowper, 1731-1800.*

There is a fountain filled with blood drawn from Emmanuel's veins;
And sinners plunged beneath that flood lose all their guilty stains.
Lose all their guilty stains, lose all their guilty stains;
And sinners plunged beneath that flood lose all their guilty stains.

The dying thief rejoiced to see that fountain in his day;
And there have I, though vile as he, washed all my sins away.
Washed all my sins away, washed all my sins away;
And there have I, though vile as he, washed all my sins away.

Dear dying Lamb, Thy precious blood shall never lose its power
Till all the ransomed church of God be saved, to sin no more.
Be saved, to sin no more, be saved, to sin no more;
Till all the ransomed church of God be saved, to sin no more.

E'er since, by faith, I saw the stream Thy flowing wounds supply,
Redeeming love has been my theme, and shall be till I die.
And shall be till I die, and shall be till I die;
Redeeming love has been my theme, and shall be till I die.

Then in a nobler, sweeter song, I'll sing Thy power to save,
When this poor lisping, stammering tongue lies silent in the grave.
Lies silent in the grave, lies silent in the grave;
When this poor lisping, stammering tongue lies silent in the grave.

Lord, I believe Thou hast prepared, unworthy though I be,
For me a blood bought free reward, a golden harp for me!
'Tis strung and tuned for endless years, and formed by power divine,
To sound in God the Father's ears no other name but Thine.

By the time I get to the end of the last verse, I have a vivid portrait of what the shed blood of Jesus has done for me, and I come away with a greater commitment to personally bear witness of His love. As I go further, and research the story behind this hymn, I discover a despairing man (Cowper), who tried to take what he thought was 'his' life in vain, only to find that 'his' life really belonged to the God who gave it. Once the light of God's love finally filled his longing soul, he was compelled to write the words of this beloved hymn, which have blessed so many. This is but one example. Other hymns such as "It is Well With My Soul", "A Mighty Fortress Is Our God", "Tis So Sweet To Trust In Jesus", "Amazing Grace", and many more, each have a story to tell that will bless us, if we will only sing them. We dare not let the hymns of the church die. We must use them in worship, and pass them on to the next generation, because they need them as much as we do. In a disquieted atmosphere, an anointed hymn can melt the stoniest of hearts, and draw in wandering minds for entrance into God's presence.

In addition to the hymns of the church, songs of praise and petitions (Psalms) are also born out of the grateful hearts and the life experiences of God's people. These prayer and praise songs provide an opportunity for believers to send up praises and petitions, individually and collectively, that express gratitude to, and confidence in our mighty God. Songs like "This Is The Day" or "What A Mighty God We Serve", unite the hearts of congregants in praise, and foster fellowship that is Christ-centered.

Then, as these melodies of gratitude and petition give way to adoration and sweet rest, songs of the Holy Spirit, or worship songs as they are called, are birthed into the spirit of God's children. Sometimes these songs have words that are understood as a part of our natural language. Songs such as "Say The Name of Jesus", or "O Lamb Of God", or "Hallelujah", allow us to exalt our God together. At other times, songs may come forth from our spirit, in our God-given prayer language. While we await an understanding of what we are singing, the Spirit of The Lord uses these songs to refresh us in the presence of The Lord. Either song, when sung from a sincere heart, according to His Word, is acceptable to the Lord. He understands all of our songs, and will reward anyone who worships Him in Spirit and in truth.

I have experienced many facets of worship in my life, and long for all of God's people to experience them as well. Therefore, it is not a burden for me to stand up and worship my God in the midst of any congregation. For, I have discovered that worship can change the atmosphere anywhere!

Preacher, as a worshipper, not only will you receive joy, peace, and healing in God's presence, but, then His Spirit will nudge your spirit, and gently entreat you to move in the direction He wants to go. If you are flexible enough to hear God and obey His Spirit's leading, God will manifest His presence and prepare hearts for the entrance of His Word, or whatever else He may want to do.

Finally, I must share this observation. Sometimes, an atmospheric change requires a redirection in worship altogether, and I may not know what to do next. In such instances, what works for me, is to simply stand up and wait on the Lord in silence. This allows time and space for God to gently gather the spirits of His people unto Himself, and speak to me. As I listen, in His own way, He places the people back into my hands for further leading.

Through personal experience, I have learned that no matter which aspect is employed, to change the atmosphere anywhere, anytime, worship will always work!

THUS LEARN:

- Every atmosphere is not necessarily set for the Word of God when you first get up to preach.
- Hymns are a very useful tool in setting the atmosphere. Learn the Hymns.
- Psalms or praise songs summon God's presence. Be a Praiser.
- Worship brings about a spiritual union of God and His People. Lead in Worship.
- Silence is an effective tool in Worship. Do not be afraid to wait on the Lord in silence.
- True Worship will change any atmosphere – anywhere – anytime – for any people. Be a true worshipper.

CHAPTER 8

SUCCESS IS GOD'S DEPARTMENT

Early in ministry, when I did not know any better, I felt the pressure to perform. I felt the pressure to produce. I felt the pressure to preach, so that I might impress my peers and the people in the pews. Alas, my true confession. God quickly put a stop to this. In my time alone worshiping God, He convinced me that there was no way I could produce at will what I had not created in the first place. He told me that I could not possibly 'preach' unless 'the real preacher' stood up in me. Jesus is the true preacher who stands up as the Holy Spirit inside of us. I finally accepted that I had nothing with which to impress anyone. I admitted that without God I could 'do' nothing. I truly praised Him for teaching me this lesson in time of private worship, and not in a public preaching setting. That would have been devastating!

As I embraced this essential truth, every time I got up to minister in any setting, I no longer felt the pressure to 'try and make something happen'. What do I mean by make something happen? For example, when the preacher tries to force a certain response from the congregation, or tries to work the crowd into a frenzied state. That's trying to make something happen.

Again, once God straightened me out, I realized that I couldn't force success in ministry. I can't make anything happen. Success is God's department, not mine. My job is to do my very best with what has been revealed to me by Him through His Holy Spirit, and trust Him for the rest.

First, I must admit that 'doing my best', does not always come automatically. It takes a determined commitment, since I do not always feel my best. In addition, because circumstances have not always been ideal, I have learned to pray in the spirit, and get into the secret place of God, so my best efforts could manifest. If I didn't feel well physically, or if the reception of my ministry was less than cordial, or if any other distraction presented itself, I soon realized that the decision to be my best was a choice I had to make. So, beloved, I made that decision. My promise to God was that every time I preached, with His help, I would push past myself and any other possible hindrances to be the best that I could be for Him.

Next, to constantly give my best, was a choice I had to make each and every time I ministered. It wasn't always easy, but no matter how I felt, or what situation confronted me, I had made a promise to myself and to the Lord, that I did not intend to break. I promised Him that He could count on me to do my personal best, and I knew He was holding me to that promise. So, half-hearted service has never been an option for me. It should not be for any of us.

Finally, I found that the commitment to be my best required 'focus'. As I kept my mind on delivering God's message, distractions ceased to have an affect on me. As I focused on The Lord completely, His Holy Spirit moved on and through me to ensure the success of His work.

I cannot say that I have the same gifts as someone else, just being honest with you and with me. But, I can say that I always strive to do my very best with what I have, and leave the 'success' to God. As I live this life of preaching, the promise to be my best has become so imbedded in my spirit, that it is easy for me to stand, no matter what, with my best effort. I find myself always praying, "Lord, please speak through me to bless your people. Unless you do it, it won't be done". Then I say amen and proceed to do my best, with the calm assurance of knowing that the success of it all is still up to Him! There is no failure in God!

By the way, as a footnote regarding success, no matter what gift seems to be needed for a particular congregation or preaching engagement, at the time of need, the Holy Ghost anointing is present in me and on me, to flow with Him as He directs. To God Be The Glory! Let Him do the same for you.

BEING MYSELF IS WHAT I DO BEST, AND IT WORKS!

Like all of us, I have a unique personality. I enjoy laughing and clowning. I am just as comfortable being very serious and somber. While teaching and preaching, I will sing, or tell a joke, if I feel led to do so. Or, I might stand silently, and just wait on the Lord. I will dress like an army soldier, or adorn myself as a bride, if it is what I believe the Lord wants. It is important to be who you are, because you are God's designer original. Imitating anyone else can only result in a limited copy. I have learned that no one can beat me at being me. I enjoy being me. Being myself is what I do best, and I have found that being me really works. It will work for you too. Be yourself!

BE YOURSELF AS A GODLY WOMAN

Secure men, are not intimidated by a strong, secure woman. In fact, secure men, are complimented by secure women. Secure, strong men are not threatened by gifted women who can come along beside them to assist. Secure, strong men, recognize help when it comes. The truth is, they are strengthened even more by a godly woman's presence.

Likewise, insecure men are often encouraged by a secure woman, who recognizes her worth and moves in wisdom. Then, many times, once a man is comfortable and secure, he becomes one of the greatest promoters of holy women.

On the other hand, no man really wants to see a woman try to emulate or imitate a man, especially when God has so wisely made her a beautiful woman. There are so many wonderful things to set women apart from men, that we women should delight to be all "the woman" we are, and thereby celebrate God's workmanship as He uses us in our uniqueness. Here are a few of the ways we can show off God's work in us.

To dress like a Godly woman gives God a chance to show off His elegance and class. To talk like a Godly woman gives God a chance to reveal His feminine wisdom. To smile like a Godly woman gives God a chance to showcase His gracious tenderness. To walk like a Godly woman gives God a chance to shine the light of His glory on His 'very good' work as we move among men. Finally, to minister as a secure Godly woman truly allows God to show Himself as the multi-dimensional God that He is. Woman of God, if this is what you want for yourself, pray this prayer with me.

"Lord, day by day, please teach me how to be the best me I can be as your Godly Woman. Help me yield myself completely to you, that I may be used in anyway you choose, and bring Glory to your name. Amen."

BE YOURSELF AS A GODLY MAN

Likewise, if you are God's Man, be a strong, secure, honest, communicative, sensitive, anointed, praying, and worshipping man. Be a man that respects and appreciates the gift of God in other men and women alike. Be a man who is strong enough to take a bold stand for righteousness, defending family and faith; yet gentle enough to bend and mold a tender plant of life if you are a father, and shoot your child like an arrow in the direction of their God-given destiny. Be a Man that women and men can happily call father or brother or son or husband or friend. Be a Man that knows who he is following, who he is leading, and that cherishes and nourishes both. Be your unique self as a God-fearing,

God empowered, and God-controlled man. Today, God is looking for Godly men who will stand tall, shoulder-to-shoulder with His strong Godly women, without intimidation or domination. If this is what you want for yourself sir, pray this prayer out loud.

> *"Lord, please help me to be a Man like Jesus was! Let men, women, boys and girls look at my life and say 'come see a man', so that I may, in turn, point them to the greatest man of all – You Jesus! Amen."*

THUS LEARN:

- Real success is measured by God's measuring rod alone.
- Trying to 'impress' men will 'mess' you up with God.
- God can do 'anything', and with Him success is assured.
- Without Him we can do 'nothing', and our failure is certain.
- Let your expectation be of God, and keep your eyes upon Him.
- No one can beat you at being you, so be the best you that you can be.
- Celebrate the uniqueness of others, in addition to celebrating your own.

CHAPTER 9

THE GLORY IS IN THE SOULS

GOD'S FAVORITE WORDS

I have met a lot of beginning ministers who believe there is a 'glory' to be obtained in being a well-known preacher who gets lots of calls and is in great demand. Well, let me help clear up that misconception right away. I submit to you that God's favorite four-letter word for Christians is not 'fame', but 'work'. Likewise, I believe that God's favorite five-letter word for what His preachers should be seeking is not 'glory', but 'souls'. God loves souls. In order to be an effective, successful preacher in God's eyes, we must love souls too. *John 4:35-36* says,

> *"Say not ye, there are yet four months, and then cometh harvest? Behold, I say unto you, lift up your eyes, and look on the fields, for they are white*

already to harvest. And he that reapeth receiveth wages, and gathereth fruit unto life eternal; that both he that soweth and he that reapeth may rejoice together!"

I thank God that He gave me a love for His Word, a love for His Work, and a love for His Harvest. Otherwise, I never would have been able to preach to a congregation of twenty, or twenty thousand with the same passion. The love of God's Word has compelled me to preach truth without compromise. The love of God's Work has compelled me to go, even when I have had to go alone. The love of God's Harvest has compelled me to labor over one soul with all my heart, until that soul received salvation. I thank God that my greatest joy was, and still is, seeing a soul come to Jesus. I know what the apostle Paul meant when he said that his crown of rejoicing was in seeing souls in the presence of the Lord. *(I Thessalonians 2:19-20)*

"For what is our hope, or joy, or crown of rejoicing? Are not even ye in the presence of our Lord Jesus Christ at his coming? For ye are our glory and joy."

No matter what the offering, or how large or small the crowd, if just one soul comes to Jesus, I can always hear all of heaven rejoicing and singing "To God be the Glory"! Preaching, for any other reason except the harvesting of souls, will often result in vain glory, and no heavenly reward.

Preaching to win souls, will always win the heart and help of God!

PREACH 'JESUS'

The truth is I am not my own. I belong to Christ. The precious blood of Jesus has purchased me. He paid an awful price to give me the gift of eternal life, through the process of being scourged, beaten, battered, bruised, and then crucified. When I consider His sacrifice, I am overwhelmed with the sense that I owe Him my all. How can I not feel the debt? I owe the Lord 'everything'. So, how can I not do 'anything' He asks me to do? I thank Him everyday for saving me. I tell Him everyday that I love Him, and I count it a privilege 'every time' He lets me preach for 'Him'.

When God sent me forth with the charge to 'preach woman preach', He very specifically told me to preach 'the Gospel of Jesus Christ'. No matter what the occasion, no matter what the audience, and no matter what the response, I was to preach Jesus. Whether preaching from the Book of Genesis, Jonah, Mark, Galatians or any of the other sixty-two books, God insisted that I dig out a picture of Jesus that would allow all to see who He is. He reminded me that the whole Bible is full of Jesus. Whether I was examining Ruth and Boaz, or David and Bathsheba, I must come away with a glimpse of Jesus. From the Word, I must somehow present His incarnation as God in Flesh, His sinless life, His substitutionary death as the Lamb of God, His burial in a borrowed tomb, His justifying resurrection, His prophetic ascension, His present-day priestly ministry, and His soon return as King of Kings! Hallelujah!

God does not want you or me to preach politics, business, economics, social ills, or injustice in and of themselves. No, we must preach the love of God as shown to us in and through Jesus Christ. Why? Because, Jesus Christ is the answer to social ills and injustice. He is the surety for all financial or economic situations. He is the consummate business partner in any venture. The Lord is the ultimate authority for law and government of all creation. Christ answers all needs of every soul for all eternity. So, God told me to simply preach Jesus and Him crucified and resurrected. Just as the Holy Spirit bears witness of Him (Christ), God told me that I should also be a witness for Christ. In addition, God promised me that those who believed me as I preached "Jesus", would receive everlasting life, and be grateful throughout all eternity for the "Good News" they had heard. That beloved, was all I needed to hear. From then until now, I have purposed to preach Christ.

I do understand that there are many subjects in the world I could explore. There are more than enough interesting people to examine, and plenty of topics waiting to be discussed from the business and political arenas. In addition, every generation does have its issues that warrant attention. Ours is no exception. But, there is no one life or subject more relevant, or precious, or powerful, or impacting, or enduring, or necessary to man's eternal well being, than that of **Jesus whom we call Christ.** Consequently, I can think of no greater job or joy, than to preach Jesus Christ and Him crucified, resurrected, and coming again – all to the Glory of God.

As a result of this commitment, in my heart I believe that I will meet many souls in Heaven who have believed the Gospel of Jesus Christ that I have preached. And, not just me only, but for every one who preaches Jesus, what a day that will be. To be sure, quite a reunion of preachers and believers will take place. Therefore, I am determined to preach Christ, for as long as God gives me breath. I pray that this will be your heart's determination as well.

EXTENDING THE INVITATION

Now, the preaching of the Gospel of Jesus Christ would be fruitless, if the invitation to come to Him were never extended. So, whenever the opportunity arises, we must always extend an invitation for sinners to come to Jesus. If you are not the pastor, as the preacher of record, be certain to get pastoral permission to extend the salvation invitation, and call to Christian discipleship. It is imperative that we as preachers remain focused on the gospel's purpose, which is to lift Jesus, that He may draw men's hearts unto Himself. To this end we 'preach', so to this end we should also 'reach'. We reach for souls, by extending the invitation to 'Come to Jesus'.

Take time at the end of the gospel presentation to ask if there is anyone who recognizes their state as a sinner, and their need of a Savior. Ask if they believe that the atoning blood of Jesus Christ was sufficient to pay for the remission of their sin. Ask if they believe in His resurrection, and whether they would like to be saved from God's judgment and eternal torment. Ask them if they would be willing to come forth, and by faith receive Jesus Christ as their personal Savior and Lord, and the gift of eternal life that He offers. Help them understand the process of repentance, and point them to passages of scripture such as *Romans 10:9-10*, or *John 1:12*, which will help them in making their confession unto salvation.

> *That if thou shalt confess with thy mouth the Lord Jesus, and shalt believe in thine heart that God hath raised him from the dead, thou shalt be saved. For with the heart man believeth unto righteousness;*

and with the mouth confession is made unto salvation. Romans 10:9-10

But as many as received him, to them gave he power to become the sons of God, even to them that believe on his name: John 1:12

There is no magical formula of words to say, because just saying words is not sufficient. The most important thing is having a sincere heart, that believes on Jesus Christ as the savior of mankind. So we, as preachers, should earnestly pray, that all who hear us preach `Jesus', will boldly confess and claim Him, as Lord of all the earth, and the Lord of their lives.

It may take a moment or two or three to minister it, but the call unto salvation that is heard and heeded, will echo throughout eternity to the Glory of God. Jesus is the doorway to eternal life. We are His ushers. Don't ever tell His story, without offering men and women the opportunity to meet Him. A final note: If as they come, you are as happy about one soul as God is, I guarantee, He will give you many more.

THUS LEARN:

- 'Souls' represents the favorite five-letter word for God. Souls are His passion.
- The whole Bible is full of Jesus. Look for Him in every story.
- Preach Jesus —His birth, life, death, resurrection and soon return —**the gospel**, for it is the Power of God.
- Always preach for the purpose of persuading men, and pleasing God.
- There is no greater way to say 'thank you' to God, for all He has done, than to proclaim Christ with accuracy, clarity and consistency.
- Preach with the same passion, to 20 or 20,000, because God is listening.
- Talk to **Him** before you preach to **them**, and never preach without praying for and inviting souls to come to Jesus.
- Celebrate every soul that comes to Jesus, and always Give God the Glory.

CHAPTER 10

ORDINATION - THE LAYING ON OF HANDS

Have you ever had an unexpected blessing overtake you and run you down? Well, ordination was just such a blessing in my life. Although I did not seek ordination, in God's time, it sought me. I did not push for ordination or even mention it to my pastor. I just kept traveling and preaching, doing my very best no matter where I went. Plus, no matter how much I traveled, serving in my local church was still a priority. I continued teaching, preaching, directing the choir, working with the youth, and whatever else I was asked to do.

I remember taking the young people to the prison to visit and play volleyball with the young inmates on Saturdays. I enjoyed taking the choir Christmas caroling in the community on cold Christmas Eve nights, followed by fellowship with hot chocolate at the church. I recall with great delight, teaching a Bible study class on Wednesdays, often to just a handful of people, and Sunday school for the teenagers whenever I was not away preaching. So, as I recall, I really did not have much time to concern myself with being ordained.

I had attended many ordination services in support of my 'fellow' male preachers. In some cases I had even helped them study for their examination. However, it did not ever cross my mind that I was being deprived of anything, or that anything was lacking. The Lord had moved me from the church of my original licensing, to another church where my gifts were being used to an even greater extent. This had opened many more doors for me to preach. By the time 1984 began, I had been preaching and serving as a licensed minister for nearly seven years. Three of which had been at this new church.

Then one day something totally unexpected happened. My new eighty-five year old bishop called me into his office. He sat me down and told me that he had been watching me serve, going in and out among the people as a Holy Woman of God. He also said that my preaching and teaching brought glory to God, and help to people in need. He went on to say that my faithfulness to the local church, and my reputation among other churches, had given me a 'good name' in ministry. He concluded by saying that the Lord had told him to set me apart to the ecumenical community, through the 'laying on of hands' by the presbytery. The participants would include a college of bishops, pastors, and other five-fold ministry gifts, in an official ordination service. I was stunned. I was humbled. I was speechless!

As I left his office, I cannot begin to tell you how I felt. I must have cried all the way home, feeling unworthy and yet grateful beyond words all at the same time. To think that God had been watching and blessing me had been enough. But to know that He had been showing someone else how to bless me, exceeded all I could have asked or thought. Now, the date had been set for a Saturday in the month of July, which was just three months away.

As I anticipated that special day, I did not know what to expect. Once again, for me, there was no formal available catechism class. I inquired, but to no avail. So, I prayed and asked the Lord to prepare me, and help me to handle whatever I would have to face.

When the day of my examination and ordination finally arrived, I stood before men and women that I admired, and had served with in ministry for years. I was brought before bishops, pastors, apostles, evangelists, and teachers. These were noteworthy preachers who sat to examine me. The examination was conducted orally, so I had to listen carefully and be sure of what was being asked. I answered every question after prayerful thought and consultation with the Holy Spirit. I answered honestly and to the very best of my ability, the Lord being my helper.

To my surprise, the examination session proved not to be a burden at all, but rather, an anointed, loving time of sharing the principles of God's Word and the tenets of our faith. After about an hour of questioning, the Presiding Bishop halted the examination and said something to me I will never forget. He said "Rita, we don't have to ask you any more scriptural questions or questions about what you believe, because we have watched you walk Holy among us. We have experienced your preaching and teaching. We know you, and we are proud to add our blessing in agreement with what God has already ordained." "So say we all"? And all the members of the ordaining council said, "So say we all"!

At that point, I fell unashamedly to my knees, in my white dress and my wide brimmed white hat. As I knelt before God, the council, family, friends and colleagues, I felt the powerful presence of an awesome God, and an innumerable company of angels!

The entire presbytery gathered around to anoint me with oil. Then they laid their holy hands on me, prayed over my life, spoke into my life, and set me apart with all the rights and privileges of an ordained elder. This allowed me to conduct wedding ceremonies, to officiate and commit the body at funeral services, and to serve the sacraments of the church. In that moment, I felt a new level of anointing, responsibility, and accountability that I believe God provided, because of His purpose, and my faithfulness.

Oh, I could say it was because of His purpose alone, but that wouldn't be honest. Why? Because, I believe the Word of God with my whole heart, and it teaches that God honors faithful service. He does not withhold any good thing from those who walk uprightly before Him. He rewards those who diligently seek Him —not just with promotion, or ordination, but with more of Himself as well.

I believe that as I sought to know Him and please Him in service, He was watching. Then, when He was ready, He allowed men to add their hands to His Hand of blessing. As a result, ever since that wonder-filled day of ordination, I have gratefully continued to do my best in giving faithful service, that the Hand of my God may continue to rest heavily upon me.

THUS LEARN:

- Ordination originates with God.
- Diligent seeking of God always brings His rewards.
- Faithful service is a pre-requisite for God's promotion.

- You won't have to blow your own horn if you blow His.
- Sincere service and study sets you apart in the eyes of God and Man.
- Seek God's Hand, and in His time He will add Man's hand.
- Verse to live by: "But, seek ye first the Kingdom of God, and His righteousness; and all these things shall be added unto you." *(Matthew 6:33).*

CHAPTER 11

THE TOWEL AND THE TELEPHONE

THE TOWEL

As the years have passed by, God has provided more and more places to preach. He has sent me to places to touch people with different beliefs, practices, worship styles and protocol. He has required that I be able to adapt to each environment and become all things to all men, that I might adequately represent Him who came to die for all men, and by His grace win 'some'.

Years ago, the Holy Spirit used a wonderful preacher, Bishop Alfred Owens, to impress upon my heart the necessity of being like a towel. *John 13:3-5.*

Jesus knowing that the Father had given all things into his hands, and that he was come from God, and went to God; He riseth from supper, and laid aside his garments; and took a ***towel****, and girded himself. After that he poureth water into a bason, and began to wash the disciples' feet, and to wipe them with the* ***towel*** *wherewith he was girded.*

A simple towel has all the attributes that the Lord needs. These attributes, when found in us, make us most beneficial in His Hands. (The traits I refer to are in bold.)

The first principle God taught me was to be **bendable** enough in my personality to take the limits off Him and His people in reference to their worship, walk and witness. This required that I learn things like the Baptist Covenant, Baptist and Methodist Hymns, Pentecostal Power Songs, the Apostle's Creed, the Methodist Liturgy and more. I also had to learn when to stand, kneel, and sit in a Catholic service. I learned which podium to use, which seat to sit in, and whether to give honor to stewards or trustees, elders or reverends, and deacons, or deaconess. In every denomination or church jurisdiction, the protocol might be different. In other words, just as a towel does not dictate how it will be used, I had to be flexible, adaptable, or bendable enough, to flow in service, no matter what might be the order.

The second principle God taught me was to be dependable. A towel does not run about the house, but remains where it is put until it is needed. A towel never says 'that's not my job!' Whatever you call upon the towel to do, it does. Whether washing the car, or cleaning the refrigerator, or fitting into a suitcase to hold down product, the towel is dependable.

So it was for me. I had to always be available to God when He had an assignment, and keep my word regarding the commitments I made. Grandmother use to say, "your word is your bond". I have found through experience that your word is directly linked to your integrity, and will ultimately affect your reputation. Dependability is part of the 'good name', that is rather to be chosen than great riches *(Proverbs 22:1)*. Hence, whenever I have made a commitment, I have done my best to keep my word. I have also done my best to be punctual, because I realize that another person's time is just as valuable as mine. Of course, at times life has handed me situations or circumstances that could not be helped or avoided, such as extreme sickness, the death of a loved one, or other disasters. However, in over twenty-five years of ministry, I can only recall missing three engagements: one because of sickness; one because of a flight cancellation, and one because of miscommunication. To God be the Glory!

Time and time again, the Lord taught me that it is just as important for me to depend completely on Him, as it is for Him to be able to depend on me. I live with the reality that without Him I can do nothing, so I ask for His help every time I minister. God loves to be depended on. I have learned that in any situation, I can depend on God, every day, I tell Him how much I need Him too!

The next principle God taught me was that I had to be **sendable**. The towel will travel wherever it is sent without question. Down to the legs, up to the arms, around to the back, the towel goes wherever the hand takes it. Thankfully, the Lord taught me how to wait on Him and then to only go where He sent me. This was essential. Through my experiences, I learned not to be anxious about God's timing. Once I was sure He called me, I knew in my spirit that He would send me out to preach.

I purposed in my heart to trust His timing, and go wherever He sent me. Remember what I asked the Lord when He first called me; to give me some place to preach? Well, the Lord assured me that He would, and I have been going every since. I have been allowed to preach in many wonderful churches, conference halls, arenas, and countless other places where hearts were waiting to hear the Word of the Lord. The key, I found, was to be **sendable**, and willing to go, knowing that God had someone there that He wanted to bless through me and His ministry.

The next principle was the importance of being **mendable** (able to recover quickly from injury). A towel does not take offense if it gets dirty or torn while being used. Neither should we. There have been times that my gender has been a major challenge to the congregation, the officers, and even the pastor. I noticed however, that this usually happened when a committee invited me. So, I learned quickly to accept invitations only from the pastor.

In those instances when I discovered that there was a gender issue, the Lord always kept me focused on Him, so that nothing which was said or done created bitterness in me. He guarded my heart with the powerful anointing to preach. Even though it may have hurt to feel the gender bias, it was often during these times that the anointing to preach was so strong that there was no doubt that God had sent me. I learned how to take it all in stride. In fact, Jesus taught me that the best way to handle offense was to forgive the offender.

I thank God He reminded me that whatever objections were being raised concerning me as a "woman" preacher, were not mine to address. He also re-affirmed that He had called me, anointed me, and sent me. In Him there was no gender issue. The Lord was only concerned with my obedience in doing what He had called me to do. This was to preach the gospel. He convinced me that the only defense I had to offer was the 'defense of the Gospel'!

Certainly, I have had to face mistreatment, disappointment, the double standard, deception and even disdain. However, the Lord has taught me not to be easily offended, hurt, or discouraged by whatever happened to me. Because I love Him so, I have always tried to be gracious, even when it has hurt. I am the Lord's servant, and He has fought my battles. I can truly say that in every situation, God was with me. He has been my glory and the lifter of my head. God cared so much about me that many times He sent someone else to encourage my soul. This enabled me to bounce back from adversity like a weeble-wobble, time and time again. Through it all, the Lord has always strengthened my soul with the reminder that my expectation was of Him, and that He would never mistreat me. This has helped me to be **mendable**, even to this day.

Finally, God taught me, I had to be **expendable**. A towel that is used today may not be used tomorrow. It may need to be washed and dried before its next usage. It may stay in the linen closet for weeks, neatly folded, and ready to be used. However, as ready as it may be, the towel cannot demand to be used.

So it was with me. I had to be willing to be used today and set on the sideline tomorrow. In my years of service, I have learned how to hand the microphone to someone else, and not be jealous or envious of anyone else's opportunity. Why? God has proven over and over again that what He has for me is for me. I now know that when I am not being used, it is a time of refreshing and preparation to be cherished. His covenant with me is that I will eventually be used again. Therefore, I count it a privilege to be a towel in the Lord's hand, because I trust His Hand and His Heart towards me. You can too!

WHEN THE TELEPHONE DOESN'T RING

Although not very often, there have been times for me when the telephone did not ring. By this I mean that the engagement invitations were few and far between. It happened more in the early days of ministry, but even as the years passed by, there were those times when my engagement book was not necessarily overflowing. As I look back, I understand that when it happened —that is, when the telephone did not ring, it was the Lord's way of giving me one of the greatest gifts of all. This was the gift of **time**! He gave me **time** to be with Him in preparation, **time** to be with myself for introspection, **time** to be with my love ones for recreation, or just some down **time** to be at rest.

At first I felt like I had done something wrong. I felt guilty for not being busy. The enemy told me that I was being overlooked or forgotten, when in fact, that was not true. As I began to reflect on the Word of God —'To everything there is a season, and a time to every purpose under the heaven' *(Ecclesiastes 3:1)* —I began to rest more and more. If God didn't let the telephone ring, or if He didn't allow invitations to flood my door for a season, it was for His reason. After all, He is my boss. So, this realization freed me to enjoy any 'time off' He gave. I even began to look at this time off, as His way of rewarding me for faithful service. He showed me that this was His way of helping me preserve myself for the journey of ministry, which will last until I see Jesus face to face.

THUS LEARN:

- Flexibility enlarges your borders.
- Dependability makes you an asset and not a liability.
- Be sent by Jesus, because if He sends you, you can go 'anywhere' and be OK.
- Keep bouncing back! Do not let offense take up residence in your spirit.
- Trust the Lord to use, and not abuse you.
- You are in Good hands—God's!

- Remember *Jeremiah 29:11, "For I know the thoughts that I think toward you, saith the LORD, thoughts of peace, and not of evil, to give you an expected end."*
- If the telephone doesn't ring don't be anxious, be thankful.
- Trust God for your schedule —He knows how much you can bear.
- Enjoy your '**time off**', because busy days are ahead!

CHAPTER 12

'OOPS'

Confession is good for the soul. Right? Ok, let's see. I confess that there have been times I have missed God. There, I've said it. What a relief. Why? Because I know I am not the only one who has ever missed the Lord. I'll bet even you have missed Him, haven't you? Go ahead. Admit it. Receive your freedom!

In my youthful enthusiasm, I remember showing up to preach at a church where the doors were locked —"oops". The church did not notify me that they had cancelled the service, and I had failed to follow-up with the saints who had invited me. I also recall showing up once to preach for a service that had been arranged by a committee, only to find out that the pastor was not expecting me at all —"oops". A major lesson was learned, since I had to be humble in the face of an embarrassing moment for the pastor and me. This was another example of poor communication, because I usually called to confirm the engagement with the senior pastor. Only this time I relied on the committee chair.

There were times when, once in service and sitting in the pulpit, I realized that I was not really sincerely welcomed. There was no peace in my spirit, no peace in the atmosphere, and no place to hide. I had to focus on God and preach through the situation. Later, I repented to God later for not consulting Him before going there —"oops".

There were places where I went and did my best. I preached all that the Lord had given. I prayed, souls were led to Christ, and the Kingdom of God was exalted. After ministering, however, I was cheated by the leadership. An offering was taken for me, but in the mind of the board members or whoever else was handling the money, there was a lack of respect for me as a minister. Consequently, the offering presented to me was far less than the offering given to me by the people. This was perhaps the most painful "oops" of all. The pain was not because of the offering alone, but because of their refusal to treat me fairly as a minister of the Gospel that was worthy of my hire *(Luke 10:7)*. Whether it as motivated by gender, or finances, or other issues I know not. One thing I do know is, by mistreating me, they insulted God.

As I went to God for comfort and consolation, He let me know that He had not sent me there in the first place — "Oops". Thank God for correction. He simply told me that it had been a test; either for me or for them, but that it was over, and I did not have to go back to minister there anymore.

Consequently, I coined the phrase mentioned earlier, "I'll go anywhere to minister once". Now, with the help of *James 4:15*, I have since modified this phrase further to say, "If the Lord wills, I will do this or do that".

ONE FINAL OOPS

Before I forget, let me share this with you. It happened relatively early in the ministry. I had been preaching long enough to establish a good relationship with many churches and pastors who would invite me back to minister again and again. In one such instance, I had been going to this particular church for about eight years straight. The Lord had blessed us each year, and this time had been no exception.

However, after service a young person came up to me and said, "Gee Evangelist, you left out a part from last year." I felt three feet tall. I had unknowingly preached the same message two years in a row to the same church. Well beloved, God was not repeating Himself. I had just forgotten.

I couldn't blame it on the Holy Ghost. This was my mistake. I had grabbed a familiar text I thought to be appropriate, without consulting the Lord —"Oops." Suffice it to say that it was a lesson well learned, even though the Lord blessed. I then started to keep track of which messages I preached and where.

More importantly, though, I recommitted myself totally to consulting with the Lord every time for every message. No grabbing! Since then, I can recall only one or two times that He has led me to preach the same message to a particular people. The difference was I knew that it was God. So did He, and so did they!

THUS LEARN:

- No one is perfect. We all miss God.
- Learn from every mistake and try not to make it again.
- Let the Lord correct and console you.
- Communication is a priceless asset.
- Remember that every invitation may not come from God so always consult HIM before going.
- Keep a record of every time you preach including the date, location, time, message given, manuscript notes, offering received, souls saved and any other comments for future reference and usage.
- Remember, no grabbing.

- Do justly, love mercy and walk humbly with thy God. This is all that God really requires, but what He requires counts most. *(Micah 6:8)*

CHAPTER 13

TO GO OR NOT TO GO FULL-TIME

All of us are as unique as a butterfly or a snowflake, so my entire ministry experience will probably be different from yours. This includes whether or not you should go into ministry as a full time occupation. Just let me say that like most things I have experienced with the Lord, I sort of 'walked right into full time ministry'. I certainly did not plan it, or set it up. I can truly say that it was the Lord's doing.

When God called me to preach, I was working full time in corporate America. I had a good paying job that provided retirement and other great benefits. I worked during the day and preached at night and on weekends. I also took vacation time to go and minister. The invitations were so numerous that often I would preach five or six evenings out of a week, for weeks at a time.

I hated to say 'no' to any people who expressed a hunger to hear the Word of God. Consequently, I would go as much as time and strength would allow. There were countless days that I would leave work and go directly to the airport, or train station, or load up the car and head out to preach. Many times my administrator met me in baggage claim at the airport coming back from one preaching engagement, only to exchange baggage and have a word of prayer with me. Then, I would fly right back out to another engagement.

My weekdays were spent completing work assignments, while listening to God for the message He wanted me to give His people. Lunch hours were used for study periods, and it hardly ever crossed my mind to go to a movie, or a club, or to say 'no' to an invitation and just stay home. In fact, I loved the work I did during the day, and I LOVED the work I did for the Lord. I kept this kind of dance going between the two careers for fourteen years from 1978 until 1992 without really thinking much about it, because God gave me the grace and desire to do both.

However, in 1990 I began to feel a struggle in my spirit. The best way to describe it is to say that I sensed that my 'job' was getting in the way of 'the work' God wanted me to do in His Kingdom. It became increasingly more difficult to focus on my daily work assignments. During the day, I found myself jotting down notes for messages and ministry, instead of looking for ways to do my job better. The corporate vision began to be less important to me than God's vision for my life, and I could no longer reconcile the two. Although the company was doing 'a good work', more and more each day I felt the need to devote myself fully to the work of the Lord. I no longer had ambitions for secular promotions or raises. I no longer looked forward to the company picnic or Christmas party. I even began to feel disconnected from my co-workers. We still got along fine, and I did my best to let my light shine before them, but I no longer had the desire or the grace to do what had been done so easily before.

So, I prayed and asked the Lord "Should I quit my job and preach full time?" His answer shocked me, because He said 'no'. I said 'no Lord?' He said 'no Rita'! Now this was a surprise to me, because I had plenty of engagements to fulfill, and I was already feeling disconnected, so it wouldn't have been hard to say good-bye! As time went on, I asked Him again, still with no release. Although I experienced an increasing frustration in having to wait, I am so glad I did not rebel against His 'no', because what happened next taught me that 'Abba, Father' always knows what is best.

In 1992, without warning, this heretofore stable company announced a 'downsizing' that would eliminate several positions —mine included. Management offered me the option of looking for another position within the company, and gave me one year to decide. When I went in prayer this time to ask the Lord what to do, He impressed upon me in my spirit to not look for any other job, but trust Him to provide for me. Oh boy! Now the real test of faith began. For so long, I had been asking the Lord to let me go into ministry full time. Now that I was faced with down sizing, was this the way the Lord was placing me into full-time ministry? Had my prayer been answered? Was I ready? Did I have enough faith? Could I trust God to provide for my daily needs? What about retirement, benefits, plus health care? I was about to find out.

During the year that I was given by the company to decide on which position I wanted, the ministry seemed to explode! I experienced increased favor from my supervisor in the form of more time off, which I quickly translated into 'more time to go preach'. I enjoyed the blessing of a steady paycheck from the job, and love offerings from the preaching. However, I gave no real thought to the future. I just spent the money as it came. I didn't save anything. I didn't know about investments, and I wasn't trying to learn. At the end of the year, following the leading of the Lord, my decision was to leave the company. With a generous separation package and a year's worth of un-employment checks ahead of me, I went merrily on my way into "full time ministry". With no daytime job, now I was free to set my own schedule, take as many vacations as I desired, and, preach woman preach!

Well, I did just that for one whole year. Then, the unemployment checks stopped coming, and I faced my first real test of faith. I had no medical insurance, no savings, and no more automatic deposits in my checking account. I had nothing to show for what I had been doing, and no 'plan'. All of a sudden it hit me that I was in full time ministry, with no one I could depend on but the Lord.

Now, He was my sole source of income. (He always had been, I just began to realize it). Now, He was my medical insurance plan. Now, He was in charge of my retirement.

Now, for the first time in my life, I understood how it felt to be completely dependent upon God for everything. I won't try to fool you. What came into my mind was "Oh God" what am I supposed to do now? As I felt my faith begin to faint, I soon discovered that He provides on the job training in faith, and grace to cover all faults and fears.

Although there was so much I did not know about full time ministry, or money management, or fiscal responsibility, He taught me as I went. Nothing was as I thought it would be. Day-by-day God taught me how to trust Him more, and how to handle what He provided. He taught me and gave me wisdom to manage the challenge of being in ministry full-time. How to manage engagements and scheduling. How to manage finances. How to pace myself while preaching. How to listen for His voice. During the early days of 'full time ministry', I gained a tremendous understanding of and appreciation for God's grace and favor. Simply because I had waited for His release, ever learning as I went, I experienced nothing from His Hand but increase!

In fact, God provided so well that my income tripled in three years, and continued to rise thereafter. I did not have to pursue engagements. Engagements pursued me. The more I preached the gospel for the Lord, the more He gave me the opportunity to do it. Beloved, I did not take up full time ministry. Full-time ministry took me up! While working with other ministries and helping others to build their dreams, I never came behind in 'any good thing'! In finances and favor, I have flourished over the years. Even still I am constantly learning from the Lord, and other great men and women, how to maximize my God-given resources, and become a channel of blessings.

Today, many preachers I know still work in corporate America, and have successful, fulfilling ministries. That is why it is so important for you to ask God to reveal His will for you, to you! Whatever God knows will work best for you is what He will lead you into, if you will acknowledge and obey Him in all of your ways *(Proverbs 3:5-6)*. Everyone is not called to give up a secular job and do nothing but preach. Somebody has to drive the buses, and process the airline tickets, and manage the restaurants, and sell the houses. Indeed, there are many preachers who work in corporate America, and have very 'fruitful' ministries. They are fruitful only because they are walking in obedience to the Lord. To go or not to go 'full time' —that is the question. God has the answer for you. Just ask Him.

THUS LEARN:

- Ask God whether you should 'Go' or 'No'.
- Don't be anxious with either answer, because He knows the way that you take.
- Wait for the Lord's release. This will always result in 'increase'.
- Remember that God takes care of His own, full time or not.
- Trust God to know what is best for you, and let Him walk you right into it.

CHAPTER 14

BE NOT WEARY IN WELL DOING

Preaching day after day, and sometimes more than once a day was and still is the joy of my life. Although it is very fulfilling spiritually, preaching can be draining physically, mentally and emotionally.

As I have traveled from place to place, many days I had to get up very early to catch a train or plane in route to the next preaching engagement. In some cases I have traveled most of the day, only to find myself waiting to be picked up at the train station or in the airport baggage claim area. The problem I have with waiting to be picked up for an extended period of time is that it makes me feel as if those who invited me were unprepared for my arrival. I must admit that this has a wearying effect on me, physically and mentally.

I remember the time a particular church sent a lady in a little red car to pick me up, and the car's trunk could not even hold my luggage. In addition, no one else was sent to help handle the bags. To say that I was weary after lifting and trying to squeeze those bags into that little car is an understatement. But, we made it!

Oh yes, there was the time a church sent a limousine driver who had no sense of direction. He did not know where the church was located, but most annoyingly kept riding around refusing to ask for directions. Because we were lost in the city for hours, I had to bypass a time of refreshing in the hotel and go directly into service. Was I weary? I'll say.

On another occasion, I missed a flight because the assigned attendant and driver were late for the early morning pick-up. Although I learned the lesson of having a backup plan B and C, it still took me almost all day to get home because of someone else's mistake. After enduring the inconvenience of it all, I was, to say the least, weary.

There have been times when I have gone to preach at churches, and they haven't even had hot water for me to freshen up with after preaching, or a warm place for me to change clothes. I hate to be wet and cold. It makes me feel weary. In some instances, churches offered no refreshments or personal accommodations. At other times, churches put me in a hotel and made no provision for food or other in-room services. Fortunately, I had my own money. However, it still made me weary.

Then, there have been those persons who anxiously volunteered to serve me. Although they had good intentions, many were overly talkative, or in need of personal ministry on the way to service. I could sense their enthusiasm, but I also knew that there was a need for proper training on how to serve an evangelist who has traveled across country to preach. Sometimes trying, but the Lord always gave me grace to tenderly share what was needed.

Finally, I will never forget the bounced church check that was never made good. This was one of the saddest experiences of all, because the reputation of the pastor who did it was completely destroyed in my mind. In addition, I suffered great inconvenience because of his lack of integrity. I made telephone calls that were not returned. I wrote letters that were not answered. I even sought legal advice regarding the option of prosecution. Trying to get a resolution to this situation wearied me greatly, until the Lord told me to "let it go and forgive him".

All of these experiences, at different times, made me feel weary in well doing, and eventually led me to pray "Lord, show me how not to be weary, and help me teach those I serve the importance of caring for the preacher with excellence. In answer to my prayer for the weariness, God gave me grace through worship. He allowed me to teach those who were willing to learn. So, if the attendant had a teachable spirit, I gently instructed on how to handle the gift that God had sent. Be sure to be on time. Be sure to accommodate the preacher when being picked up at the airport. Be sure the preacher is comfortable and safe in a nice hotel. Be sure that the preacher has adequate dinner arrangements. Be sure the attendant is sensitive enough to guard the anointing. Be sure to carry yourself with dignity and decorum. Be sure that you walk in worship as God brings His ministry gift to you. There were some people, however, that God knew were not teachable. For those persons, He gave me patience with which to possess my soul. For those churches, in some cases He simply let me know that I did not have to return.

No matter what the situation, however, God always enabled me to give my best, serve graciously, and be not weary in well doing. He promised me day after day in my time with Him, that I would reap a mighty harvest in due season if I would faint not. Beloved, God Keeps His promises! He has sustained me. Now my season has come due, and I am beginning to reap a harvest for years of patience and endurance. With a made up mind, you too will enjoy your due season of reaping. Just don't let anything or anyone cause you to be weary and 'faint' now!

THUS LEARN:

- Don't ever let them see you sweat —even when you are hot under the collar.
- Do your best, even if others fail their test.
- Guard His name and your reputation as His representative.
- Don't let your good be evil spoken of —guard your words and your walk.
- God doesn't forget your works of righteousness.
- You will reap, if you don't faint.
- No matter what, remember that quitting is not an option.
- While serving people, wait on the Lord, and He will sustain you.
- Do your part and trust God for the rest.
- Know absolutely that God Will Take Care of You.
- Guard your anointing.

CHAPTER 15

BODY GUARDS

In the early days of ministry, there were times I had to travel and preach without the luxury of having a traveling companion. I was much younger then and probably would have enjoyed having the company. Truthfully, there were times while traveling that I felt alone, and even a bit threatened by unfamiliar territory. There were some neighborhoods that were quite intimidating. In fact, I would have fainted, 'wimped' out, and refused to go, if it had not been for the peace of God which exceeded my personal understanding. Although I have more help now, a wise pastor recently shared words of wisdom that complimented the peace I had already received from the Lord. He said,

"Rita, whenever the President of the United States and his family go anywhere, they always have

the Secret Service as bodyguards with them. Whenever the Queen of England and her family go anywhere, they have bodyguards to accompany them. Likewise, in most, if not all countries, wherever royalty goes, bodyguards surround them.

Now, if these natural, worldly symbols of authority are never left alone as they go, how much more are we covered as our heavenly father's children! After all, we are the royal priesthood and ambassadors for the Kingdom of our God. Just remember the promise of God that says He will never leave us or forsake us. Keep that promise ever present in your mind. Rehearse the promise, that God gives His angels charge over you to keep you in all your ways. In fact, the angels of the Lord encamp round about those that fear and reverence and honor the Lord. Finally, know that God will take care of you, using His mighty angels who are His assigned bodyguards."

His point was understood and very much appreciated. It is wonderful to know that I am not alone. God is with me, and I travel with angelic protection. Because I now have this promise in my spirit, it allows me to come and go without fear or intimidation. I believe I have 'angelic body guards' with me at all times. For *me, this is best summed up in the* words of an old Thomas A. Dorsey chorus that says "All night, all day, angels watchin' over me my Lord. All night, all day, angels watchin' over me!" Before I go further, in light of what I am trying to communicate to you, let me say that I define 'angel' here, as a celestial being assigned to me because I am an heir of salvation, or a person or persons used by God as His tools of divine intervention on my behalf.

In fact, when I begin to think about it, I realize that my angelic bodyguards have watched over me as far back as I can remember. Once as a child, while on vacation with my family, I dove head first into a swimming pool containing only three feet of water. I hit my head on the bottom of the pool, and jumped straight up out of the water. I suffered no injury or pain. Of course, my mother testifies in jest that I have been strange every since that day. (Smile) However, we both know that it was 'God's angels watching over me'!

There was another time when Mom told me to come into the house while the yard was being mowed. Did I obey? No. Instead I hid by the side of the house to catch a glimpse of the yardman while he worked. Well, suffice it to say that we had very little grass, and as I peeped around the corner, at that precise moment, the lawn mower kicked up a good-sized rock that which hit me squarely in the left temple only inches from my eyes. My head pounded with pain, but I stayed outside and cried behind the house for a long time, because I did not want my mother to see me. I just knew I had a bruise or a cut or some other visible evidence of my disobedience. However, once again my angelic bodyguards had been at work. When I finally dried my eyes and worked up the nerve to go inside, there was absolutely no trace of any injury at all. No pain. No cuts. No kidding! I do not believe I have ever told her about it, until now. (smile). All night, all day, angels...

Lest I forget, I must tell you about one of my most memorable angelic interventions. It happened one Wednesday evening in 1998 as I was traveling out of town to begin a three-day revival. My robes, Bible, CD's and other reference books were neatly packed into my six-week old pearl white custom ordered Lincoln Mark VIII. In the middle of rush hour, it was raining so hard that I decided, to pull off the highway onto the shoulder of the road and wait for the rain to subside. I could hear one of my favorite female gospel vocalists singing Jehovah Jireh my provider, you are more than enough for me. All of a sudden, two eighteen-wheel tractor-trailers came speeding over the hill, without any regard for the rain, the law, or the road condition. Traffic had come to a halt, and stopping in time was not an option for either one of the truck drivers.

One truck completely lost control and hit the other truck causing the second truck driver to lose control and jack-knife. I watched helplessly as the second truck came sliding across a five-lane highway and totaled my new Mark VIII around me. Just before impact, all I could say was "Jesus"! I screamed His name at the top of my voice. At the point of impact, with tons of steel wrapping around my car, I distinctly remember feeling only a thump. The truck hit the car on the drivers' side, but the air bag did not deploy. The car had a full gas tank, but did not explode. The car was totaled, but I did not have a scratch! I know my angelic bodyguards were standing between that truck and me!

The Lord had protected and preserved me so well that I spent only one hour in the emergency room. The emergency room nurse was a former Sunday school student of mine, to be sure—another angel. We sang blood songs the entire time while he was examining me. I was released with no injuries. The very next morning I rented a car, repacked my things, went on to preach, and stomped on the devil's head! Alas, that Mark VIII has since been replaced with two cars, a Honda and a Mercedes Benz. All night, all day, angels...

One final but very significant instance of divine angelic intervention must be noted. Recently I accepted an invitation to minister the Word for an 11:00 o'clock a.m. and 7:00 o'clock p.m. service in Trinidad, West Indies. In my ignorance, I did not know that this is also referred to in the travel industry as "Port au Spain". So, when my travel agent made reservations for Frances and me, it didn't register with me that the destination read "Port au Prince" (Haiti). The two islands are as different as night and day.

On the day of travel, we were comfortably seated in first class, waiting for the closing of the aircraft door, when divine intervention began. Frances, who does not generally ask questions about travel, looked at the custom's declaration form, which stated 'Welcome to Haiti'. She then asked me a simple question, "what does Haiti have to do with where we are going"? This in itself could be called an act of divine intervention, because prior to closing the door, the flight attendants had already passed out the custom's declaration form. This is something that is usually done after take off. However, there we were, looking at a customs form with the aircraft door still open. So, I inquired of the flight attendant, and much to my dismay, we were on the wrong airplane! We were immediately ushered off the plane, just before the door was closed.

But wait, our luggage was left on board to fly to Haiti without us —yet another act of divine intervention. You know how tight security is these days. Security regulations normally require that passengers travel with their luggage. Our luggage could not be removed in a timely manner, but we were allowed to deplane. Why? I believe it was because God knew that:

a. There were no direct flights from Haiti to Trinidad
b. We had no place to stay or transportation in Haiti.
c. We knew absolutely no one in Haiti.
d. We spoke no French, which is the country's language.
e. Civil war had just broken out two days earlier.
f. We would have been two vulnerable frightened women.
g. We would have had to purchase new tickets back to Miami then to Trinidad in order to keep my commitment. And even then, because of the flight schedule, I would not have been able to minister at my designated time, thereby disappointing those who had invited me.

Frances and I reflected upon this potentially devastating travel glitch, we both believed it was God's Spirit, that prompted her to ask the original question concerning our final destination. So God, in His sovereign care, assigned one angel, to get us off the plane.

God sent another darling angel to help us get to our destination on time. This young ticket agent (who was supposed to be getting off work), took a special interest in our plight, and spent the next forty minutes working to solve our problem. First, he kept us from losing our return tickets to Dallas by converting them to paper tickets. Then, God let him find us two exceptionally priced round trip tickets on a flight that gave us ample time to get to the gate. Then he went home for the day. Just to show you how God works, we ended up in first class on the flight that we should have been booked on in the first place. Hallelujah!

God's next angel was waiting for us in Trinidad. Listen to this. When we arrived safely at our guesthouse it was the night before I had to minister and we had no luggage. Our luggage was in Haiti, and we didn't know how to get it routed back through Miami to Trinidad. But, God did. Our hostess was a former employee of our airline and had 'friends at the airport in Haiti'. Go figure. She called them. Right away, they tracked down, guarded, and re-routed our luggage so that we would receive it the next night. After a peaceful night's rest and an early morning shopping spree, I preached in brand new clothes and shoes. We received our luggage that night in tact. We enjoyed a successful time of ministry and fellowship according to schedule and headed home happy. Guest what? Our final encounter on the way back was also divinely orchestrated.

After we cleared customs in Miami, Frances and I headed for the gate and flight home to Dallas. As we approached an inordinately long security line, Frances suddenly began to experience a tremendous burning in her feet. (She had recently been through major surgery on her leg and foot —but it had not been a problem until now). She broke out in a sweat, and had just taken off her shoes for relief when God sent help. We were standing at the back of the line when a security lady passed by. As though by divine direction, she looked down at Frances' feet, then at her face, and asked what was wrong. After Frances admitted the truth concerning her pain and her past surgery, this woman insisted on putting her in a wheel chair. She then proceeded to escort us to the front of the line for clearance, and pushed Frances for twenty minutes to our departure gate. Upon arrival at the gate, we blessed our young angel and sent her on her way. Then, to our surprise, the boarding process had already begun. I am certain that, if we had not received such an intervention, we would have missed our flight. In addition, the strangest thing of all is that, on the way to the gate, Frances' pain had gone away as quickly as it had come! Glory to God! And it never returned! We were able to board on time and fly safely home, all the while praising God for His angelic bodyguards. As we thought of what might have been, we couldn't help singing —All night, all day, angels watching over me my Lord...

If you stop and think about it, I believe you probably have some angelic bodyguard stories too! Don't you? Well, do not be ashamed to tell your stories, because somebody needs to hear them. People need to know that angelic bodyguards are real.

Finally, I believe I still have my angelic bodyguards in this season, but the Lord has also provided His sons and daughters to assist me as I travel. God is faithful to His promise to be a keeper, and to be a company keeper! This does not mean that I can be unaware as I travel, or go just anywhere. It is essential that I be led by God in where I go, and that I have a spiritual sensitivity during each preaching engagement or trip. Thankfully, at this time, many churches also provide armor bearers and attendants who are wonderful ministry gifts. I believe this increase in help has come from the Lord, and I thank Him for it continually. I thank God that I am not alone. You know what? Neither are you!

THUS LEARN:

- Whether the lightning is flashing or the thunder is rolling —God has promised never to leave you alone.
- Whether seen or unseen, wherever you go, your bodyguards are with you, to cover and protect you from hurt and harm.
- The Lord Himself is with you so that you always have company. Therefore, you don't ever have to be lonely.
- Knowing that you are 'never' alone does not release you to go just 'anywhere'.

- Obey His voice, and only go where God tells you to go.
- Remember, someone would be blessed to hear your bodyguard stories.

CHAPTER 16

TRAVEL

Redeeming the Time

Whether traveling by plane, train or automobile, the Lord has taught me the importance of redeeming the time and making the most effective use of it as I travel. In past years, I drove to many engagements with only Jesus as my company. In those days He encouraged me to spend time talking to and listening to Him, since I had Him all to myself. So, for me, driving became my personal get away time with the Lord.

Those times of driving became times of worship and prayer. The Lord revealed so much about Himself to me, until I longed to be with Him even the more. Hours on the road provided an opportunity to spend quality time with Him. He taught me to take advantage of my time with Him. What a wonderful experiences of just being able to hear His voice without distraction.

His voice is clearer to me now, because of the time I spent with Him then. Today, I still love to be with Him in private worship, and fight for every sacred moment I can get. The principle I have learned is this: we should take advantage of every moment that we have alone with the Lord, because time in His presence is priceless!

In recent years, God has taught me that while I travel, reading, writing, and resting could prove to be far more profitable than I ever imagined. In following His lead, I have discovered that this is true. I have received so much valuable revelation while reading on airplanes. Likewise, books and songs such as "Loosed to Love", "Daddy Loves His Girls", and, even this book, have been inspired and written, while doing what I am doing right at this moment —traveling by air. In addition, I have experienced many times of restoration and refreshment while on an airplane, a train, or in an automobile, that were seemingly otherwise illusive. I enjoy a peaceful spirit, and creative thoughts flood my mind. Now, I welcome my times of travel, as if I am going on a retreat or a getaway with God!

The interesting thing to note is that lately, effective use of time has become more and more important to me. At this point in my life I try hard not to waste time, because it is one of the most valuable assets that the Lord has given to me. I take time to quiet myself, so that I can hear God's voice and receive the instructions He has for me. As I sit under the Lord through the excellent ministry of my pastor, Bishop T.D. Jakes, I am becoming increasingly aware that time is ticking away. I earnestly strive to seize and maximize each moment of my life. I must work while it is day, for when night cometh, no man or woman can work! Beloved, for each of us, night is coming! So, we must take advantage of any moment God gives us to cherish Him, and use the gift of time wisely.

GOOD ADVICE

My life is truly a walk of faith. Every time the phone rings and an invitation is received and accepted, it is an act of faith. I never really know what I will walk into, or encounter from day to day. One day the crowd is more than anticipated. The next day, it may be a total disappointment for the one who is hosting me. Although many may have contracts or agreements that guarantee them a certain dollar amount no matter what the size of the congregation. God has not led me to do so. I give my best and trust God to move on the hearts of those who invite me, to obey Him and bless me. Most times they do. Sometimes they don't. It's all about faith.

As I go from place to place, I pray and get on airplane after airplane as an act of faith. Even getting into cars with strangers (something my mother taught me never to do) requires child-like faith every time I am picked up and transported to the hotel and church service. Here are some tips that I believe will help as you travel.

First and foremost, pray for a joy-filled journey and a safe arrival. Always verify your travel arrangements with your host ministry or make your own, to ensure that the itinerary provided will work for you.

Packing –

1. Study your assignment and decide which clothing and resource materials are needed at least 2 or 3 days ahead of departure.
2. Take care of any washing or cleaning of clothes and robes at least 2 or 3 days ahead of departure.
3. Be sure to allow for a change of clothing after each service.
4. If you are going to more than one location, the change of clothing properly cared for can be used more than once if you just wear it before and after preaching.
5. Use travel size toiletries to conserve space in the luggage.
6. Invest in good luggage, and do not over pack it.

7. Carry shoes that can be used with more than one outfit in order to save space.
8. Check the weather for where you are going and prepare to dress accordingly.
9. Take lots of Vitamin C if you are going to be exposed to extreme changes in weather.

Airports –

1. Give yourself at least one and a half hours to navigate through check-in and security. Allow two hours for foreign travel.
2. Always have a plan 'B' for getting to the airport so you won't miss your time of departure.
3. Wear simple non-metallic clothing whenever possible, plus easy to remove shoes for security screening.
4. Keep all medicine that is required daily with you in your carry-on luggage, purse, or briefcase.
5. Re-check any tickets with the appropriate carrier to confirm the itinerary.
6. Be sure you give yourself more than enough time to make the scheduled departure.
7. Do not presume that commercial carriers will wait for you. They will not.
8. Always have a plan A, B, or even C to ensure your positioning for departure.

9. Learn the unique characteristics or rules that are related to the different airports or train stations. For example, Hartsfield Jackson International in Atlanta is one of many airports that require to you to navigate your way within a given time line through several steps in order to get to the departure gate. Knowing these steps and pacing yourself accordingly is vital to success.
10. Just in case things happen, such as very late departures or missed connections, it helps to have a good book or some work you can do or, a good friend so you can talk. Any one of these can help you maintain a positive attitude in situations you cannot control.
11. It is also advisable to have an emergency fund (cash or credit card) with you just in case you become stranded and have to pay for an overnight stay, or purchase an unexpected ticket home. A *working*, widely accepted credit card can be helpful if you do not like carrying extra cash.
12. In this time of heightened security, be patient and very cooperative with all professional security personnel no matter what mode of transportation you use. Jokes are not funny, and rebellious or riotous attitudes will delay you, at best; and, at worst, may cause you to be detained or possibly even locked up.

13. Remember the word of God says in Romans 12:18 *"If it be possible, as much as lieth in you, live peaceably with all men."*
14. Use the professional approach. Be cordial and cooperative for best results, even when you are rudely treated. In this case the official is 'always right'. Remember; "Be not overcome with evil, but overcome evil with good" *(Romans 18:21)*.

Room stay –

1. Make sure to request a secure room with room service whenever it is possible.
2. At check-in time, make sure you have the only outstanding keys to your room.
3. Check A/C or heat to make sure it works.
4. Check bathroom for working plumbing.
5. Review the emergency escape route.
6. Make the room as comfortable as possible, and secure all personal valuables.
7. Make sure someone back home knows the number to where you are staying.
8. Get sufficient rest to enable you to minister effectively. Quiet time with the Lord is so important. Shopping can wait.

THUS LEARN:

- Time misspent is time lost, and time lost is difficult to regain.
- Time well spent is an invaluable investment that reaps unlimited dividends.
- Time well managed in travel becomes a good friend.
- While traveling, redeem the time: reading, writing, resting and worshipping.
- Time is a gift use it wisely.
- Walk by faith, but know as much as you can before you travel.
- Think the trip through as completely as you can.
- Be prepared for the unexpected.
- Pray without ceasing.
- Praise the Lord for every safe trip!

CHAPTER 17

TAKING CARE OF MYSELF

When you're young you think you will never get old. You believe you will be able to run through troops and leap over walls forever. The Superwoman, Wonder Woman, Cinderella syndrome says, I am faster than a speeding bullet; more powerful than a locomotive; and, I always will be the belle of the ball. When I was twenty-five I can assure you I felt this way. I ripped and ran, up and down the highways, over the rails, through the air, with little sleep.

There were also many times I lifted and tossed heavy baggage without a second thought. Often, I would leave a church after preaching, with a wet, uncovered head and an exposed neck. I had no regard or real respect for the temple of God, whose temple I was. I didn't mean myself any harm. I just believed I was invincible. Oh, the ignorance of youth!

I can remember my grandmother saying to me years ago, "Rita, don't read in the dark; you will mess up your eyes". Did I listen? NO! So, today, my eyes are in need of a miracle or some strong glasses. Surely, God can perform the miracle I need, yet why should He have to give me a miracle? Yes, glasses are available, but maybe wearing them could have been avoided, had I listened.

Or did I obey when my grandmother said "cover your head and neck, Rita, so you won't suffer years from now"? Did I take heed? NO! Now my neck and shoulders are paying the price. I find myself grappling with joint pain, praying yet again for healing. I realize now that this also could have been avoided.

Finally, did I listen when my own mother said, "Rita, get your rest, because you cannot make up for lost rest"? NO! Oh how I wish I had. Being rested helps one to be much more effective. Please, beloved, do not make the same costly mistakes I have made. Take care of yourself!

I'm doing all I can do now, but wish I had taken heed long ago. Things would be so much easier today, if I had made healthy living a lifestyle from the beginning. But I didn't, so recently I have had to adjust my life considerably, and make room for things like proper rest, a proper diet, and exercise. These things don't come naturally to me. I have to work at them. I have finally discovered that living a healthy life is based upon a decision we make, and our commitment to follow that decision. There is no magical cure for neglect. Re-setting of priorities and reconditioning of my behavior is required. I also know that the success of this process depends upon my confession (how I speak), and the action I take (exercise daily). So, recently I have begun to eat right, exercise, and tell myself over and over again that I am worth it.

I AM WORTH IT!

I used to believe that everyone else was important but me. I loved to please people. I considered everyone else's happiness before mine. I even believed that serving the Lord and working for Him was a 24-hour, 7 day a week job. If I wasn't going off to preach, I was getting ready to go preach, or just coming back from preaching. Ministry was not just my calling. It had become an obsession —a god. I didn't really understand the 'abundant life' Jesus came to give me.

As a result of this imbalance in my life, I experienced what is known as 'burnout'! I say burnout, because the fire and desire of ministry had all but died out in me. My life had become a laborious routine without joy. Day after day I continued packing, traveling, preparing, preaching, returning and unpacking. I did all this without even stopping to smell His wonderful roses. I had gone week after week, month after month, and year after year, without a vacation. I only took days off if sickness necessitated it. The truth is, I had been working for God —not with Him. All the time I thought I was doing the Lord a service, but in reality, I was doing a disservice to Him and to myself. I never realized that He cared more about "me" than my ministry.

Oh, how I thank God for using many special people He placed in my life to help me discover that — 'I am Worth It'! My best friend told me. My mother and father told me. My brothers and sisters in ministry told me. My Pastor told me. The Spirit of God told me. Now, although it has taken some time, I finally realize this essential truth. I am important! I am worth it!

My health and well being matter too! It is okay for me to sleep in —to take a vacation – to go to the park or go fishing – or go bowling or watch a movie. I don't have to feel guilty about getting a massage every week if I want one, or buying something new just for me! Wow! Thank God, I finally 'get it'! Now I understand that the blessings of the Lord make us rich, and He adds no sorrow with them. *(Proverbs 10:22)* Beloved, all of God's riches cannot be counted in dollars. Living well can be counted as riches. Being healthy definitely must be counted as riches.

Taking care of myself has become my personal battlecry, because I have discovered something very important about myself. I really do love me. God loves me, and I love me too. God wants abundant life for me, and today I can truly say that I want abundant life for me too. Why? Because I finally realize this priceless truth; Jesus died and rose again just to let me know "I'm Worth It!" Guess what? This truth is meant for you as well. If you haven't already done so, please receive it, and take care of yourself because you are worth it!

TRANSITION

Now that I have preached for a quarter century, I find myself in transition. There is an intellectual shift taking place in my reflection on ministry. I contemplate far more seriously every move I make. At the age of fifty-four, my physiology is changing. I am experiencing a divine makeover!

The ministry God has given me is also in transition as it moves into another dimension. One result of the transition in my ministry has been a re-evaluation of my methods. This includes the expectations I place on myself as well as those that I serve. I have been told many times by my peers that I am too easy, thus, setting myself up to be abused. They say this because they know that in past years I have not required any special consideration for myself. Because I wanted so much to be a blessing to the churches I have served, I never asked for first class travel, or companion tickets, or special hotels, or even attendants to help me with my luggage. No contracts were sent, and no honorarium was set. I wanted to serve the Lord by serving His people, and I trusted His people to appreciate and bless me as the ministry gift of God. This I have done all of my preaching life.

As I pause in honest reflection today, I must confess that a modification of methodology has become necessary. Why? Because even though there are many churches and pastors who have recognized, honored, appreciated, and taken excellent care of me, many others have taken advantage of God's grace and gift. They have invested as little as possible in the invited ministry gift, while expecting the greatest possible move of God in return. Many have spent time choosing flights requiring two or three connections instead of a direct flight, just to save money on the ticket. Some others have paid for room and tax only at the hotel, with no meals or room service included. Still others have been down right stingy in sharing God's financial blessing with God's servant in the offering or honorarium.

Therefore, I have sought the Lord in this, and He has shown me what to do. I am to help the people of God take better care of me, and thereby set them up for a greater blessing from Him. He told me to tell them the things that will make it easier for me to minister effectively. So, today I let ministries know my requirements as the Lord leads, and re-enforce those requirements whenever necessary.

Please know that what satisfies and works for me may not be sufficient for you. My suggestion is to seek the Lord regarding ministry requirements, and let Him tell you what to request and require. Don't just emulate others; listen to Him! As you do, He will keep you from being abused, and from becoming an abuser!

Interestingly, God has recently revealed new streams of potential income. He has also filled me with creative ideas and strategies that will bless me and others now, and in the future. He wants me to be set financially, so that I can give abundantly to kingdom building. He is teaching me how to work smarter and not harder, that I may glean all He has for me. He will do the same for you if you ask.

STRETCHED BUT NOT STRESSED

I have learned the importance of being 'stretched' without being 'stressed'. Growth requires change, and change is hardly ever convenient or comfortable. I have moved from being just an evangelist on the road, to pastoring, teaching, evangelizing, and running two businesses at the same time. Consequently, I have had to willingly adapt to each environment, and work to master every God-given assignment, without succumbing to its possible pressure or stress. I believe that God is looking for this kind of flexibility in all of His servants today.

Being 'willing' is a personal decision each of us must make. *If ye be willing and obedient, ye shall eat the good of the land (Isa. 1:19).* This is a matter of choice. In other words, our blessing is contingent upon our obedience. This is not rocket science since we all know that obedience is better than sacrifice *(I Sam. 15:22).* Our obedience, more than anything else we might give, releases the planned blessings of God upon our lives.

I must take a moment and address the 'adapting' part. No longer can we, as His ministers, be one-dimensional in our willingness to serve. If a worship leader is needed, the preacher should be able to lead in worship. If a simple facilitator is required, the preacher should be humble enough to maintain the flow of the service without overstepping the boundaries of the assignment. If teaching is the order of the day, the preacher must be ready and able to teach the Word of God. If prayer and body ministry is called for, the preacher of God should be armed with prayer, and have a sensitivity to God's Spirit that will allow the Lord to have His way. If preaching is it, the preacher must always be able to preach the Word with power and authority! In business, God's servant must exemplify the greatest work ethic and integrity as His representative.

In other words, today's servant of the Lord should be able to flow in whatever is needed, without feeling stressed. Hint: This is only possible as we learn to rest in the Lord, and wait patiently for Him! I take Psalm 37 regularly, for prevention of stress attacks!

> *Fret not thyself because of evildoers, neither be thou envious against the workers of iniquity. For they shall soon be cut down like the grass, and wither as the green herb. Trust in the LORD, and do good; so shalt thou dwell in the land, and verily thou shalt be fed. Delight thyself also in the LORD; and he shall give thee the desires of thine heart. Commit thy way unto the LORD; trust also in him; and he shall bring it to pass. And he shall bring forth thy righteousness as the light, and thy judgment as the noonday.*
>
> *Rest in the LORD, and wait patiently for him: fret not thyself because of him who prospereth in his way, because of the man who bringeth wicked devices to pass. Cease from anger, and forsake wrath: fret not thyself in any wise to do evil. For evildoers shall be cut off: but those that wait upon the LORD, they shall inherit the earth. For yet a little while, and the wicked shall not be: yea, thou shalt diligently consider his place, and it shall not be. But the meek shall inherit the earth; and shall delight themselves in the abundance of peace. The wicked plotteth against the just, and gnasheth upon him with his teeth. The Lord shall laugh at him: for he seeth that his day is coming. The wicked have drawn out the sword, and have bent their bow, to cast down the poor and needy, and to slay such as be of upright conversation. Their sword shall enter into their own heart, and their bows shall be broken. A little that a righteous man hath is better than the riches of many wicked. For the arms of the wicked shall be broken: but the LORD upholdeth the righteous. The LORD knoweth the days of the upright: and their inheritance shall be for ever. They shall not be ashamed in the evil time: and in the days of famine they shall be satisfied. But the wicked shall perish, and the enemies of the LORD shall be as the fat of lambs: they shall consume; into smoke shall they consume away.*

The wicked borroweth, and payeth not again: but the righteous sheweth mercy, and giveth. For such as be blessed of him shall inherit the earth; and they that be cursed of him shall be cut off. The steps of a good man are ordered by the LORD: and he delighteth in his way. Though he fall, he shall not be utterly cast down: for the LORD upholdeth him with his hand. I have been young, and now am old; yet have I not seen the righteous forsaken, nor his seed begging bread. He is ever merciful, and lendeth; and his seed is blessed. Depart from evil, and do good; and dwell for evermore. For the LORD loveth judgment, and forsaketh not his saints; they are preserved for ever: but the seed of the wicked shall be cut off. The righteous shall inherit the land, and dwell therein for ever. The mouth of the righteous speaketh wisdom, and his tongue talketh of judgment. The law of his God is in his heart; none of his steps shall slide. The wicked watcheth the righteous, and seeketh to slay him. The LORD will not leave him in his hand, nor condemn him when he is judged.

Wait on the LORD, and keep his way, and he shall exalt thee to inherit the land: when the wicked are cut off, thou shalt see it. I have seen the wicked in great power, and spreading himself like a green bay tree. Yet he passed away, and, lo, he was not: yea, I sought him, but he could not be found. Mark the perfect man, and behold the upright: for the end of that man is peace. But the transgressors shall be destroyed together: the end of the wicked shall be cut off. But the salvation of the righteous is of the LORD: he is their strength in the time of trouble. And the LORD shall help them, and deliver them: he shall deliver them from the wicked, and save them, because they trust in him.

Find out what prescription works for you and take it!

THUS LEARN:

- Take time for you —'**me time**' —and do the things that refresh you.
- Let people help you, because it is really help from God!

- Pay for the services that you need and can afford (household maintenance, yard landscaping, hair, cleaning, cooking, etc.)
- Let the skycaps and bellmen lift the bags, and reward them accordingly.
- Get your physical rest, and let your spirit rest in the Lord.
- Drink plenty of water – it is God's medicine.
- Eat right and exercise.
- Believe that you are 'worth it'.
- Don't worry —be happy —Live a full and happy life!
- Don't be afraid to define your needs as a ministry gift.
- Be open to transition and change.
- Stretch without being stressed!

CHAPTER 18

RELATIONSHIPS

There are great rewards in relationships. Friends are special. Family and friends are essential for our emotional health and well-being. They help to keep us in balance. This is especially true for preachers who are involved in daily ministry. If we are not careful, we will lose our focus on the simple companionships that God places in our lives to keep us in harmony with Him and ourselves. When we are blessed with relationships that move beyond mere causal acquaintance, we can develop as well-rounded individuals.

Those relationships that develop into close friendships give us that time for pleasure without pressure. Like any profession, preachers need a place of laughter and rest. We need that quiet place that builds self-esteem, where intimate friends share devotion, respect, and understanding. We are in need of a haven that will allow our creative talent to flow freely.

One suggestion for success in ministry is to have someone who is older than you are as a friend, who, in fact, may become a spiritual mentor. This should be someone who can share the sensible wisdom of God. There is a blessing in making friends with older people, for they will usually tell you everything they know about life. Such is the case with grandparents, or Godparents, or spiritual parents. They will sharpen you, polish you, and cause you to stretch professionally and spiritually. Be led by God; He will show you their heart. As you listen to and obey Him, you will grow.

Another suggestion is, be open to develop friendships with your contemporaries. Remember, however, that intimate friendships take time, and wisdom and discretion should govern your confessions. You share your faults, failures, and faith with these intimate friends. They know your dreams and can pray you through your temptations, or just go to the movies or a basketball game with you.

I have a few relationships that started out as just acquaintances but, then evolved into wonderful friendships over the years. I stay in touch with these friends. I see them as often as I can. I enjoy their company whenever we get together, and we know that we can count on each other for love and prayers and support, as it is needed.

I also have a loving, close-knit natural family. We have an awesome time whenever we get together, and we try to make that as often as we can. Mom and Dad are older now, so I make it my business to get home much more than before. When I do get home, I love on them with all my heart. Many times I just to call to tell them how much I appreciate all they have sacrificed for our family. I listen to glean priceless gems from their wise lips. I pray for them without ceasing. In addition, I do my very best to 'be there' for my two sisters, three brothers, and their children, whenever the need arises. We spend very special times together like Christmas and birthdays. Although we may not see eye to eye on every subject, I am blessed by my relationship with each of them.

I also have an extended family of surrogate children and grand children that light up my world. On any given day, I am 'Grammy', 'Auntie Pastor', or 'Mama T'. I love it!

I have found out the hard way, however, that there is only one me. I must finally admit that I cannot be in two places at once. As much as I would like to be three of four people at the same time, there is really only one me. Now, I am a good me. I am a loving me. I am a generous me. I am a funny me. I am an adventurous me. I am a playful me, but I am still only one me, and there will be no clones.

Anyway, in spite of this limitation, I can still say I love me. I like me. I enjoy being with me. I make me laugh. I am okay crying with me. I am the president of my own fan club. Believe it or not, enjoying this self-love has made me a better, more loving, and more loveable me. It has also brought about a `great' peace in my life, and helped me in my relationships. I no longer worry or fret at all about who loves me. Who likes me? Who believes in me? Who is for me? Who will help me? Who wants to be with me? Or, any other `who'? What then are we to say about these things? If God be for me, who can be against me? *(Romans 8:31)*. I know that God is for me, and I am for me too! This has become the most liberating and empowering feeling in the world. I owe it all to the love that God has given me for me.

But again, as much as I love me, there is still only one me to share in all of my relationships. So, I sought the Lord on how to manage my relationships. In response, He is showing me daily how to regulate the attention and care I give each one. The Lord has made it easy for me, because each day He will whisper what to do in my ear. Sometimes He says `call this one', or `send this one flowers', or `take this one bowling', or `go to lunch with him', or `buy this toy', or 'call and go by', or whatever. And it works every time. When I listen to God and obey, there is never a schedule conflict, or missed opportunity to grow the relationships He has given.

Quality time spent with a person, just being myself, has proven to be the most important ingredient in cultivating strong, lasting, fulfilling relationships. There is absolutely no substitute for time, and I am extremely grateful to God for an understanding of this major truth. I have also discovered that I cannot wait for nurturing moments to always present themselves. Instead, I have to take the initiative, and pursue every opportunity to nurture these precious relationships. Time management is a vital key, and I thank God for teaching me day by day how to manage my time wisely. Books, tapes, and seminars on time management do help, but God is my greatest teacher. With His help, it is not a burden to work on my God given relationships. The result is that I always receive much more than I give. As days go by, I realize more and more that investment in relationships now will pay off wonderfully in the future.

On the other hand, I have learned when to re-evaluate a relationship. This is something wisdom teaches. From experience I can say preacher, beware! At times you may find yourself dealing with someone who has a constant sad story, someone who wants you to take care of them, or at least wallow with them in their self-pity. Don't wallow. Be prayerfully led in helping, but ask God to show you when enough is enough. Do not allow anyone to distract you, or take you off of your God-given course.

Then again, some people might try to use their knowledge of you when you had nothing. They want to make you feel ashamed of your success and God's blessings. Misery often loves and seeks company. Don't listen to them. You dare not apologize for the success that God provides. Trying to please everyone who may have known you 'when', no matter what 'when' means, will keep you from being happy with the blessings of the Lord in your life 'now'.

Also, take a hard look at anyone who is not happy for you, or cannot weep and rejoice alike with you. They probably don't really love you. Remember, no amount of money can buy love. You cannot make people love you, like you, or treat you right. It must come naturally, or it will not last. The key, I have found, is in loving yourself. When you love yourself, you will not hurt yourself, or allow anyone else to continually hurt you. In God's wisdom, He made it a commandment to love Him and to then love yourself, because He knew how much we would benefit from proper self-love. He also knew that loving Him and loving ourselves would enable us to love one another correctly.

As I continue to reflect on the rich relationships in my life, my very best friend, Frances, comes to mind. For over twenty-seven years, God has used her mightily in prayer for me, and in many other practical ways to help me become a better person. Frances taught me honestly, and patiently, how to coordinate or 'hook-up' outfits, jewelry, shoes and hairstyles. She also encouraged me to start saving money, instead of spending every dollar I received. This enabled me to build a new house. When I get frustrated, she is there to remind me that just one moment in God's Kingdom will pay for it all. We have enjoyed so many wonderful times together laughing, singing, traveling, shopping, eating, and even caring for each other's family. Of course, over the years, we have had our ups, and downs. Sometimes we have even asked each other the question "did God really tell us to be friends?" The answer has always been yes. Both of us have worked to cultivate the relationship, while not allowing it to hinder any of what God has told us to do as individuals. This is everything true friendship should be.

Now, Sandra wears the hat of lawyer, colleague in ministry, and friend. This presents a unique challenge in that we must separate each aspect of the relationship in our mind and operate in the role that each arena requires. For instance, as pastor, Sandra is submitted to me in her role as an elder and teacher. As her client, I am submitted to her for counsel and legal advice. As friends, we fellowship with and support each other as much as we can. Whether traveling in ministry, or eating out, or taking care of loved ones, or going to basketball games, or tackling homeowner projects, church issues or legal problems, we have learned to regulate the different facets of our relationship and benefit from them all.

Next, LeRonn and Steven are friends and colleagues that I feel comfortable hanging out with anytime, anywhere. They treat me like the queen that I am, and I treat them like the kings that they are. We know that we are there for each other, and we make it a point to stay in touch and get together as often as we can. When we do, we have great fun.

Then there is Angelene, who is a doctor and friend and confidant and prophet and exhorter all rolled into one magnificent wife and mother. She reminds me to take time for myself when I would forget. No other people – just 'me' time. I sure do appreciate her soft, empathetic, yet firm voice that helps to keep me healthy. Even though we are both very busy in our professions, we find time to do dinner or concerts or other enjoyable activities when we take our 'girls time out'.

For certain, my surrogate children, grandchildren and God-nephews, and nieces teach me a lot about cultivating and regulating relationships. I have learned in child psychology from Ricky Jr., Rachel, Jordan, Timothy, Christian,

Joshua, and Annie that you don't give one child a gift if all are present, without giving a gift to all of the children. Sometimes a gift can be a hug. When it comes to giving attention, I have learned that; whether I am wrestling with Jordan and Timothy, or listening to Annie, or having a tea party with Rachel, or playing catch with Ricky Jr., or singing lullabies to Christian, or throwing Joshua in the air, I had better be rested enough, to give each one of them the time and energy which will say that they are important to me. Needless to say, I have to be in shape!

For the adult surrogate children in my life, I spend as much quality time as I can with each of them on a personal basis, and as a family. As a pastor, they don't mind sharing me with the rest of the body of Christ —in and outside of the church. In fact, their respect for me in ministry is most encouraging.

Although it might not be the case for every preacher, my natural family is a tremendous source of inspiration to me. Mom and Dad Mosley, whose comments are at the end of this book, have encouraged me all of my life in everything I have endeavored to do. I remember asking for a flute when I was just six years old. It was the first of many requests that would follow. (Boots, uniforms, class ring, school pictures, prom gown, gas money, rent etc.) Although money was tight at the time, my Dad found a way to buy the flute and bring it home, even though he knew I would drive them crazy, making strange noises as I learned to play. A couple of years later, someone stole my flute. At first I was afraid to ask for another one. Finally I let Mom know, who told my Dad, who went right out and replaced it. I play the flute to this day. All my life Mom and Dad have spoiled me so rotten, it's a wonder I don't stink (smile). There are no words to say how much they mean to me.

Then there are my siblings: Sharon, Jackie, Vaughn, Virgil, Chris, and their children Joy, Alisha, Kara and Tyler, whom I love so dearly. Before God gave me wisdom, at times I put our relationships under a strain as a preacher, because they didn't always appreciate me preaching to them every time we got together. Of course, as I look back, I can't say that I blame them. At Christmas, I preached. At family cookouts, I preached. For birthday celebrations, I preached. On family vacations, I preached. I'm surprised they didn't shoot me. I was such a church nag, until finally my friend Frances told me that I was driving my own family away from me and the Lord. She wisely counseled me to just love them, be a good sister, let my light shine, and let the Lord do the rest. I did! He did! And today, my saved brothers and sisters are some of my most ardent ministry supporters. Whenever we get together now, we have so much fun it is simply awesome.

Lest I forget, there have been loved ones God has placed in my life as priceless treasures I could never have afforded, and would not have traded for anything in this world. Aunt Delores, who is with the Lord now, prayed me through many a battle, and always, I say always had a word of faith to deposit when my soul was despairing.

Then too, Uncle Bobby's words have kept me encouraged many a day. No matter how bad things looked, he would always say, "everything's gonna be all right". That's all he said, and that was enough to see me through.

Isabella, or MaBelle as we call her, is a continual wellspring of wit and edification. She is forever building my self-esteem. When I feel my worst, her words "Rie, Rie, you look so pretty"; make me lift my head, square my shoulders and walk like I know I'm looking good. And her most emphatic word to all of us is always "after you've done all you can, what are you gonna do? That's right. You Just Stand!" Everybody needs a 'MaBelle' in their life. I'm sure glad God gave me mine.

God knows I can't leave out the Twiggs side of the family. I really love my aunt Hallie, my biological father Coleman, my cousin Helen, my sister Coleman, my cousin Hattie, my cousin Mary, my cousin Connie, cousin Howard and the rest of the Twiggs clan. Although I have just gotten to know them recently, it seems like we have known and loved each other forever. Whenever I see cousin Helen, I just want to hug her and never let go. Everybody needs a cousin Helen to hug and be hugged by. When I see Aunt Hallie, who is eighty plus years old now, I just want to sit at her feet and listen. So I do!

Finally, the matriarch of the family, Mom Mary, who was my paternal grandmother, went to be with the Lord some years ago. However, before she died, I met her. Let me share the story with you. It happened on a trip I had taken to find my biological father (her son Coleman). I was about forty years old. I had successfully located him in Houston, Texas with the help of a dear friend, Johnny B. On the way to meet him, we stopped off in Temple, Texas. Johnny told me he had a surprise for me. First he took me to see my father's brother, uncle Connie —and then he took me to see my grandmother, Mom Mary. She was a beautiful woman with long silvery hair, but could no longer see. Now this was the special part. She had not seen me since I was a baby. However, as soon as I stepped into the room, although she couldn't physically see me, when I opened my mouth and said "Hello Mom Mary", she said "Reedy? Is that my Reedy?" At eighty plus, she recognized the voice of the forty-year-old granddaughter she had never heard speak before. Only God! What a moment! I will never forget the look on her face, or the sound of her voice as she called my name.

As you can tell, I have been blessed with wonderful relationships. I know that I am not alone. I have taken the liberty of telling you about these special people, and I hope I haven't bored you with my life. I have shared these stories with you, believing that you have some wonderful relationships too. Why do I say this? Because God doesn't love me any more than He loves you. I know there are some relationship treasures in your life that, if you would take a moment to examine, are priceless and precious!

Take a moment. Think about it. Let the memories run across your mind. Stop and smell the roses in your garden of friendships. If they are past relationships that have blessed you, give God praise for them. If they are present relationships that are blessing you, give God praise and nurture them even the more. If they are not blessing you, give God praise and ask Him to help you re-evaluate them. For future relationships that God has waiting to bless you, lift those hands, give Him praise, and be ready to receive them!

THUS LEARN:

- Relationships should be inspired by and initiated as God leads.
- Cultivate your relationships as directed by God.
- Evaluate of relationships as signaled by God.
- Good relationships should be cherished and nourished.

- There are great rewards in relationships.
- Friends are special; they help keep us in balance.
- Family and friends are essential for emotional health and well-being.
- Thank God for good relationships.

CHAPTER 19

SISTER TO SISTER

I commend unto you Phebe our sister, which is a servant of the church which is at Cenchrea: That ye receive her in the Lord, as becometh saints, and that ye assist her in whatsoever business she hath need of you: for she hath been a succourer of many, and of myself also. Romans 16:1-2

For many years I have heard it said; "a woman's worst enemy is usually another woman". Whether in everyday life, or in ministry, women have been marked as those who envy, backbite, undermine, and in general do not support each other. Of course, there are several possible underlying causes, which might go from one end of the spectrum —pride and inflated ego, to the other— low self-esteem and insecurity. Whatever the cause, it is time for us as God's women to change our "reputation". I believe that the prescription for a successful turnaround is found in scripture.

In this passage, the Apostle Paul who has been given credit for writing over seventy-five percent of the New Testament, sends a letter to the Church at Rome (we know it as the book of Romans). He does not use Barnabas or Timothy or Peter to deliver it, but a woman named Phebe. As he writes, he commends her to the saints. He tells them to receive and assist her in whatever way she may have need of them. Why? Because, she is a sister, a servant, and a succourer or benefactor of many. Today, as twenty-first century women of God, we should do no less for each other. We must be benefactors and selfless servants:

1. Knowing that we are sisters through the blood of Jesus, and that our sisterhood is by His design.
2. We should celebrate each other's gifts and talents. We must be willing to assist each other in life and in ministry.
3. In the natural, sisters share dreams, clothes, secrets, support, and more. Likewise, we who are sisters in Christ should be able to trust each other with our secrets and our dreams.

We also must assist one another, and provoke each other to be all we can be in Christ. In the natural, sisters do not choose each other. Neither do we choose each other as sisters in Christ. We are given to each other by God, and should strive to be an absolute blessing to one another.

Paul next encourages us to receive and assist each other, because we are servants of God. As female servants, we have often labored and sacrificed behind the scenes, with little or no reward or refreshment. Therefore, our common bond in this area should foster a greater appreciation for each other, and increase our sensitivity to each other's need for help. We should come to each other's rescue without ulterior motives. It's not enough to say, 'If I can't help you I won't hurt you'. No. We must find a way to help one another!

Finally, we are admonished by the apostle to assist the 'succourer' in each other. Now, a succourer is a benefactor, a missionary, or one who shows a needed kindness. Her bounty is extensive. She is one who gets you ready for the race of life. She is also someone who helps prepare you to do your best, and will do it in the background. In other words, a succourer could be classified as the wind beneath your wings.

Women of God, the conclusion is that we, more than any man, should have each other's back. We should have each other's back in prayer, and in preparing each other to take the stage of life and be successful. Why? Because we're family. God's family. The church family. The blood-washed family of Almighty God. We have a heavenly Father that we all share. As such, when one succeeds, we all succeed. Therefore, we should be willing to coach each other, correct each other, comfort each other, and count on each other. Once we learn to do this as sisters in Christ, I believe God will use us —His mighty women, even more effectively as 'helpmeets' to His mighty twenty-first century men.

Not only will it shock the world, confound the enemy, and unite the church, but it will please our God who spoke the command through His apostle in the first place. So, what was that command again my sister? Let me summarize it in five simple words: Take Good Care of Phebe! This is God's Word of challenge to us as His twenty-first century women. Frankly, I believe we are up to the task!

PHEBE HELPED ME

Here is how the 'Phebe' principle works.

It is a truth that we are perceived, and many times judged to a great extent, by what we wear. For a long time before I received help from God-sent Phebe, people were laughing at me. They weren't laughing at my ability or anointing to preach. They were laughing at my attire. Behind my back they were whispering and making fun of the image I was projecting. I don't blame them. Now I understand their reason.

At that time, I would alternate and wear one of three suits I owned; with my one pair of non-matching stacked healed shoes, no make-up, no matching jewelry and a bun on my head. I also had this one wool coat I wore year round. Here is how it went. I would preach in a suit at church numbers one. After preaching, I bundled up in my coat and sat in the pulpit until the benediction. Then I would go sit in my car and let the suit dry on me; go to the church number two, and preach in the same suit.

People laughed at and talked about me, but no one offered me any help, until one day I preached at the Church of the Holy Trinity in the District of Columbia. After the message I bundled myself as usual in my trusted coat, went to my car to dry off, and, would have gone on to the next church, when I heard someone say "Rev. Twiggs, may I speak with you for a moment?" It was a young lady named Frances. I said "yes." She then took the time to honestly share what I needed to hear. Later, she counseled me on the latest fashions and took me under her wings as a Phebe. From her I learned that attire does matter. As I applied what she taught, from that time forward, people stopped laughing at my attire, and perceived me differently.

After that, I preached in suits (and hats) for years, until one day the Lord spoke to me. He told me that in some services I needed to make a distinction between the congregation and myself by wearing a robe. I complied and commissioned robes to be designed for me. Then, He proceeded to tell me when to wear a robe, and when to wear a suit. To this day I still ask Him what to wear when I go to preach. As I do, I am always dressed appropriately for whatever service I am attending. For regular church services, when I have to preach, I usually wear a robe. For workshops and seminars, I usually wear a business suit. For conferences, I wear a dress, or dress suit, or robe, as I am led. I ask, and God answers with peace. I have never regretted His leading, nor forgotten the help He sent through His Phebe.

THUS LEARN:

- Sisters are a gift from God.
- We are family —sisters in the Lord.
- As women, we can change our reputation.
- Servants should not be taken for granted.
- Succourers or benefactors should be celebrated.
- Be a blessing and you will receive a blessing.
- Be willing to give and receive the help God sends.
- Attire does matter. Listen to God.
- Take good care of Phebe.

CHAPTER 20

MENTORING

More and more these days, I am asked to be a personal mentor by male and female ministers alike. Instead of saying yes or no right away, I take their information and tenderly say that I will get back to them. Not because I don't want to do it, but because I believe that a personal one-on-one mentorship, or any other style of mentoring must be ordained by God. As it was started for Elijah and Elisha by God in *I Kings 19:19-21,* I believe God initiates the mentoring connections for me as well. Let me explain.

Approximately fifteen years ago, I met a young woman who was getting started in ministry. What I presumed to be just another casual acquaintance proved to be nothing of the kind. In a way, which only God could do, He knitted our hearts and then instructed me to mentor her.

At first I hesitated, because I did not really have a clear definition of mentoring. I had heard the word tossed about here and there but had no idea what it really required. Nevertheless, I was willing to learn, and of course God was more than willing to teach me. The process that He revealed to me one-step at a time, first required one-on-one ministry exchanges; whereby iron could sharpen iron. Another step included creating space in my life for her to shadow me in my daily walk, as I fulfilled my ministry schedule.

In obedience to the Lord, I granted her access to my life. We spent many hours getting to know each other as women and as ministers. We shared the Word of God, food, fun, fellowship, dreams, and visions. We prayed for and encouraged each other, and the Lord blessed our times together tremendously. Often, as she traveled with me to engagements, we sat in silence on the way. Once we arrived, I would preach and she would do whatever I asked. Then, on the return trip we would discuss all that had happened. I answered her questions to the best of my ability, and poured as much of what I knew into her as the Lord would allow.

One of the most significant periods we spent together was during a season when I did a leadership training series for a particular church. It was in the dead of winter. The classes were scheduled for twelve consecutive Monday nights in a city approximately thirty miles away. Every Monday she was ready to go, on time and eager to learn. Some Mondays the weather was so inclement that, like Elijah, I would call and tell her to stay home. But, like Elisha, she would insist upon going. As it turned out, those bad weather days provided some of the most anointed times of sharing. Near the end of the series, I allowed her to team teach with me. She proved to be more than capable of handling the assignment. Then, because she had done so well as a team teacher, I allowed her to teach a class by herself while I observed. She did a wonderful job. Although I critiqued her, she received it with gratitude. This spoke volumes to me.

After this experience, the Lord allowed me to recommend her for invitations that I could not accept. In every case, she rose to the occasion and represented the Lord with excellence. As her gift began to make room for her more and more, and my schedule became even busier, approximately one year after it began, the season for one-on-one mentoring came to an end.

We continued in prayer and fellowship as time allowed. We talked often by telephone. Little by little, it became apparent to us as well as others that the mantle of the Lord that was upon me, was also upon her. Today, approximately ten years later, she stands as one of God's finest preachers—Pastor Jasmine Sculark. Many who hear her minister call her my daughter. Frankly, I do too. Just last year her father in the ministry, Dr. Charles Booth, and I served proudly as she was installed to the pastorate of a prominent church in York, Pennsylvania. This year, both he and I returned to join in celebrating her first pastoral anniversary. The church is growing and thriving under her leadership, and she is still gleaning information from us both as her mentors. Although the planned one-on-one segments ended years ago, the process of indirect mentoring has still continued for more than a decade.

Beloved, let me say here that the Lord has not instructed me to personally mentor anyone else in quite this way to date. Even though I enjoy sharing whatever I can, whenever I can, with whomever I can as the Lord allows, it has not been to such a personal extent. In teaching settings I have been able to instruct, correct, reprove, and even rebuke those who have had a desire to know, and a heart to receive. By the same token, I am told that many preachers, male and female, young and old, black and white, have gleaned much concerning ministry from me through observation, even though it has been from afar.

Please understand that observation is not to be underestimated. In fact, this is one way I have been able to experience mentoring. There are those with whom I walk together in spiritual agreement, but our daily paths do not always cross. Hands-on training is not practical. Personal attention is not always possible, or even necessary. I have found that observation, and impartation by precept and example, are two of the strongest, most effective tools in mentoring. I have also discovered that sometimes, distance allows you a broader and more insightful view. As you watch carefully, you learn lessons that God does not ever articulate verbally. I have the joy of observing a wonderful Bishop. With a nod, he speaks volumes. With a peak over his glasses, he can correct and comfort at the same time. I have gained wisdom as much from his silence as I have gained from his words. As he pursues his dreams with passion and excellence, I am inspired and compelled to pursue my dreams as well. I have studied the way he thinks, so that my thought process can be strengthened and enlightened.

These are not treasures that are passed lightly in moments of fellowship. No, these golden nuggets must be mined patiently, and gained primarily in obscurity. Fortunately, what God has allowed me to treasure privately, He uses in public.

I am a product partly of all of the private mentors I have ever had in ministry. Pastor Sidney Yancey, who gave me the opportunity to preach that `first official sermon'. Pastor David Durham, who stood outside after church sharpening me with the scriptures. Pastor Robert Williams, who gave us young preachers somewhere to go, and let this young eager woman preach in his pulpit. Bishop Arthur Christian, who set me apart for ordination. Bishop Ralph Dennis, who, as a father affirmed the apostolic anointing that is upon my life. Bishop Ernestine C. Reems, who sets a shining example for all women in ministry. And, Bishop T.D. Jakes, Sr., who, as father and mentor, installed and trusts me as pastor. I can't help but praise God everyday, for the treasures He has made available to me through His wonderful goldmines.

Much that one learns is from impartation. The same is true for anyone who wants to learn from God's men or women. So it must be for those who would be mentored by me in this season of my life. Unless the Lord specifically says so, I do not believe time will permit the same one-on-one to hands on approach I once used.

Now, even though it may require observation from a distance, it is my prayer that the messages I preach, the precepts I teach, and the example of my life in ministry will provide a level of impartation in mentoring for those who would walk in spiritual agreement with me. My advice to you preacher is, discover the treasure that God sets before you, and dare to mine!

THUS LEARN:

- Mentoring should be initiated by God.
- No matter what heroes you may have, worship God and don't allow anyone to worship you.
- Mentoring is a process over time.
- Mentoring requires honesty and transparency.
- Mentoring requires spiritual agreement.
- Mentoring does not always equate to friendship.
- Mentoring does not necessarily require continuous one on one ministry.
- Observation and spiritual impartation are major mining tools in mentoring.

CHAPTER 21

A NEW SEASON

ANOTHER ASSIGNMENT

As the new millennium came in with the year 2000, I experienced a change of assignment from the Lord. For twenty plus years, I had served the Lord as an evangelist, preaching and teaching the Gospel nationally and internationally. Then in 2001, God promoted me to my new assignment. This assignment was to pastor His people. Although I had no previous experience, God let me know that He had been preparing me all along for His promotion.

So, when my Bishop confirmed the shift, I had to make some necessary adjustments to my schedule and priorities. God did not take me completely off the road, but for three years, I had to balance my time on the road with my new responsibilities as a pastor of the flock. Today, I can truly say that God has given me grace to do both, with love, peace, and great joy.

FROM WHERE I SIT

Many people sit on the outside and have a misconception of what the inside of ministry is really like. Let me share the view from where I sit. For me, being a pastor underneath a bishop presents a unique challenge. How so? I am glad you asked me.

First, as the only female pastor along side several male pastors, it is absolutely imperative that I maintain a balanced, sensitive relationship with each pastor and his wife. Holiness and wholeness have to be the hallmark of my interaction within this inner circle. Thankfully, because my motives and intentions are pure, it is not difficult to be at ease with and relate to each pastor and his wife. Through acknowledging and honoring both, I have gained the honor and respect of each one. I must genuinely care for their children as well.

Next, I am the first daughter. I am not the first lady. Nor am I one of the guys. I am constantly looked to as a role model in the areas of attire, attitude, actions and ministry. In other words, I am expected to "represent" the women as a lady, while still flowing in a spirit of excellence, as I carry my part of the load along side the brothers.

As an under-shepherd, I must love and care for the flock of God as my own, while remembering always that they do belong to God. God taught me in the beginning as an Evangelist, to gather the flock; first unto God, then unto the Senior Pastor. Because I learned this lesson early, it was not difficult for me to add guarding and guiding to gathering. This is what I do now as an associate pastor. I still gather the flock unto God unto His appointed Bishop, while serving as guard and guide and caretaker for them. This involves teaching, counseling, consoling, correcting, challenging, weeping, rejoicing, marrying, burying and much more.

Although I am an extension of the Senior Pastor, I must also be a watchman and intercessor for him and his family. For me, pastoring is both a job and a joy. It has its privileges and it problems. It comes with frustration as well as fruit. Although the buck does eventually stop with the Bishop, the complaints, compliments, and challenges will usually make their way first to the pastors. Handling either complaint or compliment, requires the grace of God.

Finally, being an associate pastor affords me the opportunity of learning. I don't carry the full weight of the ministry and its success. However, I do affect its success. It is like being an apprentice. I get to learn without having to worry about paying the bills. However, I treat the bills as if they were my own. This is the stewardship I have learned.

Although it may sound strange, I believe that God has provided an even exchange for me, in that I receive as much as I give. As a bonus, God uses our Bishop to constantly preach life changing messages. If that were not enough, we who are under the skirts of his garment, are graced to receive special assignments, continuously, that teach life and ministry lessons, which have become more and more valuable to me day by day, from where I sit!

PAY ATTENTION

How many times have we as individuals been exposed to greatness, and not taken advantage of what we could gain —just because we were not paying attention? I dare say that the voices of many gifted men and women have often gone unheeded, leaving valuable lessons unlearned, because we as God's people have not paid attention.

Whether it is because we believe we know it all; or we are too busy to stop and take notice; or we have our own idea as to who we believe can help us, not paying attention to all God sends our way can be very costly.

Knowing when to be silent and listen is a tremendous asset. Many times I know I have missed priceless gems and nuggets, while using my mouth instead of my ears. Since I learned its importance, I have gleaned so much from listening. I listen not just to good preachers, but to gifted orators from all walks of life. In my experience, politicians, doctors, lawyers, bankers, teachers, chefs and countless others, have provided wisdom and knowledge as I have listened to them speak. Certainly, being observant of others in and outside of ministry has proven to be priceless in the exposure it has provided. Having such a reservoir to draw from has enriched my life, and hopefully enhanced my contribution to the people I touch. Hearing is something we do without effort. In order to really listen, however, one must pay attention.

I believe this brief note has been a much needed reminder from God to all of us, letting us know that paying attention is so much better than paying the cost of its alternative —which is ignorance or limited knowledge. So beloved, the next time the opportunity presents itself in word or deed, please count it as a wise investment to pay attention!

COMING FULL CIRCLE

I share this story with you, in hopes that it will encourage your heart, increase your faith, and strengthen your resolve to trust God for your times and seasons.

Twenty or more years ago, as a rookie female preacher, I attended the Hampton Ministers Conference in Virginia. It was the premier preachers' conference of that day. Some of God's finest preachers in the world were presented, and they preached extraordinary messages to what seemed like an innumerable multitude of eager, hungry, rookie preachers and seasoned veterans alike. At the time, it was known as the 'country club' of preaching. The quality of preaching and teaching was second to none.

Women, however, were not included in the line up of preachers. In fact, they were a rare commodity. Ironically, as I attended, I never felt like a sore thumb or fifth wheel. My brothers in the 'fellowship' (remember the fellowship?) attended as rookies also, and treated me like a rose among thorns. Year after year I sat in awe, just imagining what it would be like to stand where those mighty preachers stood. I dreamed of one day being able to address that august body.

As time marched on, my own preaching schedule prevented me from attending the conference as much as I would have liked. Although I ordered the tapes, I still missed the dynamics and the experience of actually being there. Yet, the dream remained. I still claimed to myself, that one day I would stand as a keynote speaker to this wonderful gathering of preachers.

Now, fasting forward twenty plus years, by God's grace, the first female president of this formerly male dominated conference was installed in 2003. Dr. Suzan Johnson Cook is the name of this pioneering, preaching woman who has been selected by God to lead the Hampton Ministers Conference into its next dimension. As an inspiring colleague, a special sister, and a well-prepared torchbearer, this woman of God is leading the way for women preachers and teachers with courage and grace.

When I received the invitation to come and share in support of her inauguration, I was extremely honored, but also reminded of my dream. There she was; this supremely educated, faithfully proven, gracefully articulate, seasoned warrior woman, being inaugurated as President of the Hampton Ministers Conference. As I sat in that service, I realized that God had chosen to use her as a doorkeeper, and as an usher for many. I rejoiced with her as we witnessed the changing of the leadership guard. Oh, it gets better!

A few weeks later, I received a call from President Cook that brought tears to my eyes and joy to my heart. My dream was about to come true. In that conversation she invited me to address the conference. My God, My God! All I could think of was that God had brought me full circle! He had answered yet another prayer!

Well beloved, with God's help, in 2004 I stood where many great preachers before me had stood, including, my very own dear pastor. God allowed me to fulfill another one of my dreams. I stood upon the platform, and spoke from behind the podium of the Hampton Ministers Conference!

As I did, I was very mindful that there were other young dreamers sitting there at the beginning of their preaching journey, as I had been more than twenty years before. My prayer for them was that they would be encouraged to keep their dream alive, and pursue it until it became a reality like mine. I knew how they felt, because I had 'sat where they now sat.' I earnestly prayed to be a blessing to them on that day, and the Lord did bless, —as I came full circle!

THUS LEARN:

- Recognize the shift in seasons.
- Pay attention so you don't have to pay for ignorance.
- New assignments will come with new and sufficient grace.
- Understand and appreciate your God-given place.
- Serve the flock as a faithful steward.
- Don't be afraid to dream, because dreams do come true.
- Never give up on your dreams.
- Real pioneers hold the door open for others.
- Be thankful for and supportive of God-given pioneers.
- You will come full circle.
- Don't forget to be a blessing as you come full circle.

CHAPTER 22

PEARLS OF WISDOM

Before I let you go, let me share some pearls God has given me in my times of mining and meditation.

GIVE NO PLACE TO JEALOUSY

There is no good thing that God will withhold from us as we walk uprightly before Him. Psalm 84:11. In other words, if we walk right before God, there is no limit to what He will give! In addition, because of our position in Jesus Christ, we have been given permission to ask God for 'anything' in Jesus' name, and have full assurance that we will receive it. *John 14:4.*

Why then would we envy anyone anything, when everything is ours for the asking? I believe that the seed called envy, which is often born out of pride, contaminates the spirit and grows into a disease called jealousy. This selfish disease can destroy your witness and short-circuit your blessings. So many cruel and hurtful things are done out of a jealous heart. I can speak from experience, because there were times that I had given in to a jealous or envious spirit myself. Let me say that it robbed me of joy, peace and productivity. I could not focus on what God was trying to give me, because I was too busy comparing myself and envying others. I measured other preachers' popularity against my own. I compared what I thought they had to what I had, not knowing a thing about them or what they really possessed (all those I's were messing me up.)

God quickly gave me a much-needed revelation. He told me that I had no idea what the other person's life was like, or the trials that might have accompanied their blessings, or what price they paid to get it. None of us really know the price someone else has paid to be who they are. My jealousy was an ungrateful spirit in the sight of God, and His Holy Spirit did not hesitate to convict me of it. I am so glad He did. Why? Because it released me to receive all that He had for me. Because I now recognize the complete potential and personal blessings that are mine, this has freed me to rejoice sincerely with others in the blessings they receive, and enjoy what God has given me even more. I can walk in peace, joy, and productivity, because jealousy has no place. I am so glad God delivered me from the spirit of jealousy. I pray that if it is needed, you will be delivered too.

PUT AWAY CHILDISH THINGS

We don't have time to play with toys of sin. The only time we have left, is time to do right. We don't have time to drag our legs in laziness. We don't have the luxury of waiting for someone else to do what God has told us to do. For certain, every immature characteristic we find within ourselves should be put away right now, so that the virtues of our God can be revealed in us.

The time has come when we must live what we preach and teach. We must teach and preach what God's Word says, without favor and without fail. There can be no compromise for us as mature sons of God, because Jesus is coming so soon! When I was a child (immature in the spirit), I did childish things. I played and wasted precious time and energy. However, as a sincere servant of the Lord, I am older now (wiser and more committed). Though it has not always been easy, I thank the Lord for helping me to continually put away childish things, so that I may hear Him say "Well Done", when He comes again!

I'VE GOT YOU

Once I was walking with my then two-year old God-nephew, Jordan. As a new walker —he was taking fast and excited steps. When he came to a curb he stumbled and would have fallen, but I was holding his hand. He looked up at me with those little trusting brown eyes and I said, "Jordan, I've got you!"

Friend, this is what God wants us to know. We don't have to worry about taking any steps in any arena, even as 'new walkers'. We don't have to be afraid of the risky curbs, because even if we stumble, He won't let us fail or fall. Beloved, I have Good news from the Lord. God told me to tell you that He's holding your hand and 'He's got you'! He's got your back, He's got your front, He's got your family, He's got your finances, He's got your future! So, go ahead. Take exciting steps. Walk without worrying. Run in spite of the risks. Do it without doubting. Why? Because God says, I've Got You!

TURN AROUND AUNTIE PASTOR

At three years of age, God gave Jordan yet another truth to share with us. I was sitting in my office one Sunday morning with my back to the door, just typing away on my laptop. Suddenly, I heard a small voice say, "Auntie Pastor". I recognized the voice and said, "Yes, Jordan", but never looked up. Again, he said "Auntie Pastor". I again answered "Yes, Jordan", as I continued to type. Three times he called my name and received the same half-attentive response. So he made up a song right on the spot and sang: turn around Auntie Pastor, turn around. Turn around Auntie Pastor, look at me.

I was so stunned by his creativity, I whirled around in my chair, and looked into his little dancing eyes. He smiled with great joy, knowing that he now had my undivided attention. In that moment we shared a special connection. Immediately, it was revealed to me that this is what our God is seeking from and saying to us in all of our hustle and bustle —turn around sister such and such turn around. Turn around brother busy man look at me. If we do, we will experience His smile, and an exchange of great joy! Thanks Jordan!

LIFE IS GOD'S MARATHON

Once we get into God's will for us (our lane), we must discipline ourselves, and run with patience the race that He sets before us. We must look unto Jesus who is the author and finisher (coach and editor) of our faith. As life shifts, different ages and different stages require adjustments on our part. Only God can help us learn what it will take for us to finish our course successfully and with joy. God can help us keep our faith in tact, as we run the long and relentlessly demanding marathon of life. Seek the Lord. Enough said.

GROWTH REQUIRES CHANGE

Growth requires change, and change is hardly ever predictable or convenient. Therefore in order to grow, I have had to be a willing change agent. I have had to be adaptable to any environment, and able to master any assignment given. God is looking for this kind of flexibility in His ministers today. No longer can we be one-dimensional. We must be 'stretched but not stressed'. As noted earlier, if worship is needed, the preacher should be able to lead the congregation into worship. If teaching is the order of the day, the preacher must be able to teach. If preaching and body ministry is God's purpose for the moment, the preacher should have no difficulty flowing in whatever gift is needed. In addition, we should be constantly seeking, and open to ever increasing technology for usage in spreading the Gospel. Being this flexible will allow God to grow us without limitation.

JUST STAND

It's not always about progress or immediate success, but endurance. A wise old man once said, 'what cannot be remedied, must be endured." Other wisdom teaches, when you deny people their struggle, you deny them their strength! MaBelle says, "after you've done all you can, just stand!" I say, if you get knocked down, pray, and God will help you to bounce back up again, and land on your feet!

DON'T STOP LEARNING

There is a dangerous temptation that is subtle but fatal to the preacher, or any one else for that matter. It is the temptation to be satisfied with where we are, what we have learned, and what we have accomplished. When we yield to this temptation, we become guilty of the sin of complacency. Now, once complacency sets in, it is very easy for 'good' to become an enemy to 'better', and for 'better' to become an enemy to 'best'. When we become satisfied with good, we no longer push ourselves to do better. If we settle for having done better, we rob ourselves and others of the best that is in us. I know God is never satisfied with less than our best, and I know He doesn't want us to be satisfied either. Preachers need to be the best representatives of Christ.

One of the quickest ways to become complacent is to stop studying. Why? Because continued study serves as a catalyst for growth and motivation. The more we study, the more we will know. The more we know, the likelihood is that we will do more. As preachers, I have come to realize that the water of the Word in us must be living, growing and flowing, in order for us to be open water hoses of life to others.

As much as I know this to be true, now more than ever, I have discovered that a concerted effort must be put forth on my part every day to maintain personal motivation for study.

Over twenty-five years ago, intense discipline in study came naturally to me. There was such a desire to know everything about God, because I knew that I did not know anything. I studied all the time and learned a lot. Now, twenty-five years later, I must confess that ongoing ministry and perceived success, has opened the door to the temptation of complacency. Admittedly, I have been tempted to rest in what I learned years ago.

However, the Lord has emphatically convicted me for closing the door of my mind to increased knowledge. He will not permit me to limit or stunt the growth of my effectiveness in ministry for today and the future. He has reminded me that continued growth, or 'taking in', is just as much a part of my stewardship as 'giving out'. In fact, if I don't continue to learn, very soon I will not have anything fresh to give. I must hunger enough to eat continually, or I will not be able to continually feed others who are hungry. I thank God for this revelation: In order to lead and feed in the market place, I must continue to come and dine in His secret place.

MINISTRY THROUGH CRISIS

There are times in a preacher's life when we must go and minister in the midst of personal crisis. None of us are exempt from tragedy, heartbreak, health issues, family issues, age issues, or any other issues that may arise. I have been asked the question: "What do you do when crises arise in your life, pastor?" As best I can say it, here is my answer. Taking every day one day at a time is the first thing I do. Each day I believe I am given new mercies, and a grace from God to face whatever will come my way. I also believe Him for strength to function and be content in whatever state I am in, whether in ministry, in business, or in my personal life.

Because of my love for the Lord and His work, I am able to focus my attention and energy on 'doing in spite of'. In the meantime, I also take my burdens to the Lord in prayer and leave them there. When my heart is overwhelmed, I run to the rock that higher than I. This rock is Jesus. Do not underestimate the power of your relationship with Jesus, because it will be the anchor you need to hold you in the midst of any one of life's storms.

Hold fast to the words found in *Mark 4:35*, where Jesus tells His disciples "Let us pass over to the other side".

When they woke Him up in the midst of the storm, He calmed the wind and the waves, but rebuked them for their lack of faith. Why? Because He wanted them to remember and trust His words. "Let us pass over to the other side". His words could not fail. Through storm or unclouded sky, Jesus had said that they were going to the other side.

As I embrace this lesson, and constantly remind myself (in the midst of any storm) that 'Jesus and I are going to the other side', the storm no longer has the same affect on me. I enjoy heaven on earth with Jesus. Worshipping God, while trusting His Word, as simple as it sounds, is what I do when any crisis arises in my life. This works for me, and I believe it will work for you too!

THUS LEARN:

- It is very hard to cry over someone else's blessings while counting your own.
- For all that any of us have, a price has been paid —even if it wasn't paid by us.
- Get busy claiming your own 'stuff' from the Lord, and be thankful.
- Rejoice with others and someone will always rejoice with you.
- Playtime is over —it never really existed anyway.

- Procrastination should be avoided at all cost, because it costs so much in the end.
- Turn around and look at God.
- Make full proof of your ministry now —you will only get one life to do so.
- The more we study, the more we realize what we don't know. And that's a good thing.
- Do not get stuck on good or better, but strive to be your best at all times.
- In crisis, worship God and believe His Word!

CHAPTER 23

A FEW "RITA" MOMENTS

THANK GOD FOR THE HEARTS OF MY LIFE LONG MENTORS – MOM AND DAD

"I believe Rita had her first calling when she was about four years old. One Sunday while the choir was singing and before the sermon, Rita left her mother in the pew, walked up on the pulpit and sat beside the preacher. She seemed to be right at home. Later it was revealed that she felt at home with the choir as well. Now she is a singer and a preacher.

Then, when she was about eight years old, Rita was required to recite a scripture from the Bible. It was quite a long and trying request, but she recited the verses perfectly. The entire church was rather spell bound by her accomplishment.

Rita was always a rather fascinating child. One year, when she was about nine, her elementary school was putting on a Christmas play. Rita had one of the minor roles, which required very little participation; however, a day before opening night, the lead player became ill and did not show up for the play. I can't remember the role. It might have been either the role of Joseph or Mary. Anyway, since Rita had practiced every day for the play, the teacher asked her on the opening night if she knew the lines and could play the role of Joseph. Rita stepped right in, and that night a star was born.

Rita lived what seemed to us to be a rather strange life in later years. She would give anyone the shirt off her back. She gave strangers a lift when her car was running, and even invited strangers into her home for shelter or a meal. She was extremely benevolent to outsiders, but always found time to come visit the family in Indiana or wherever we were stationed. She would load up on food, clothing and money (that girl would wear her stacked heel shoes down to nothing). With the help of her dear friend Frances, we finally got her to move from high water pants into dresses, suits and nice high heel shoes.

At times life was tough for her, but she loved living for the Lord. It was there in Washington D.C. that she received her final call into full time ministry. She would preach to a congregation of three as long and as hard as she would to a congregation of three thousand. She has had a long row to hoe, but we believe that she has weeded the garden well. We are extremely proud of her and love to hear her preach the gospel." Lovingly submitted by Pearl and Virgil Mosley!

CHAPTER 24

SET UP TO LEARN

Over the course of this writing, I listed various lessons that I believe are relevant for anyone in the preaching ministry. In order to be an effective preacher, you have to, at least, pray and think about *the calling,* what is required in order to position your self to go forward to full-filling it, and how God wants you to accomplish His will for your life and ministry. Yes, many are called, but few are chosen. If you believe that you are among the chosen, then take another look at the lessons and learn.

Chapter 1

THUS LEARN:

- As a preacher, you must 'know' in your heart of hearts that you are **called** of God.

- A human witness may encourage you, but even if no man bears witness, the Holy Spirit and the Word of God must bear witness with your spirit.
- Remember that we make plans, but God's purposes prevail.
- Pray for God to open the doors of opportunity; to provide the message; and to guard His message.
- The infilling of the Holy Spirit is a priceless asset and glorious experience. Enjoy Him daily.
- An intimate relationship with God helps prepare a preacher as an effective spokesperson for Him.
- Yield to God's Spirit and receive all that He gives.
- Answer every call of God for your life.

Chapter 2

THUS LEARN:

- It is important to talk with your pastor or his/her designated appointee, if you believe you are called to preach, or even if you are not sure.
- Be patient but persistent in pursuing your meeting with the pastor.
- No matter how painful it may be, submit to your pastor's decision.

- Remember, the prejudice of men does not override the purpose of God.
- Stay planted where God has put you, and bloom where you are planted.
- Know that your promotion comes from the Lord.
- The heart of your pastor is in the hand of the Lord, so pray.
- Trust God, because your times and seasons are also in God's Hands.
- Know that God will allow you to be released in His time.
- Study to be ready when your time of release comes.

Chapter 3

THUS LEARN:

- Do not go on your own as a beginner. Please wait to be released into ministry.
- As a minister who is just starting, do not assume that you know anything about preaching.
- Pursue your pastor for guidance in preparing to preach. If classes are available, welcome them.
- Ask questions about everything when you are not sure. The only bad question is the question you do not ask.
- Following your pastor's guidance, prepare an outline from your study notes.

- Review your message with your pastor.
- Practice preaching your message from the outline to yourself in the mirror and others, if they will listen.
- Practice will help relax you and allow you to be yourself.
- Know that God is the only one you have to please, but do work to please Him.
- Take criticisms, counsel and compliments alike to the Lord.
- Let God's voice be the final voice you hear and obey.

Chapter 4

THUS LEARN:

- God's calling on your life is not dependent upon you, your feelings, or the feelings of others.
- God will not hand you more than you can handle.
- Do your best with every God-given opportunity.
- Be reminded that Jesus will reward all of us; so strive to be the best you can be.
- A lump of coal, no matter how hot it is, will cool off quickly if it is left alone.
- Always listen to, and glean everything you can from good preaching.
- Pursue fellowship with good preachers.
- Be willing to give and receive support as a preacher.

- Know that good fellowship can result in lifelong friendships.
- Never forget that 'fellows' in the 'ship' need each other for the trip.

Chapter 5

THUS LEARN:

- God has the message. It is our responsibility to seek Him, and prepare ourselves as the messenger.
- People do not care how much you know until they know how much you care; so let the love of God show wherever you go.
- God taught me personally that if I put a price on preaching, I would be putting a limit on Him. However, if I would trust Him to provide, He would be an unlimited source of abundant supply.
- Stay under pastoral covering and remain faithful to work in your local church, even as you go out preaching.
- Love God, love His Word, love His people, love His work, and you will always have job security in His Kingdom.

Chapter 6

THUS LEARN:

- Paying dues earns one the right to be honored, and there are no short cuts.

- Be quick to sow seeds of honor. They will come back to you as a mighty harvest.
- Remember in protocol, it is important to know 'who to call'; so do not be afraid to ask.
- Communication with the pastor is essential to success in any church. Call to ensure agreement regarding customs, order and expectations. When in doubt, take the conservative route.
- Do not mess up another preacher's house. One day you may have your own.
- Be a blessing through protocol, and you will receive many a call.
- You do not get a second chance to make a 'first' impression.
- Take care of the hands that take care of you. Say 'thank you' —it lingers in the mind and waters the heart.
- Pay close attention to the details of protocol.
- Humility costs you nothing, but arrogance can cost you everything.

Chapter 7

THUS LEARN:

- Every atmosphere is not necessarily set for the Word of God when you first get up.

- Hymns are a very useful tool in setting the atmosphere. Learn the Hymns.
- Psalms or praise songs summon God's presence. Be a Praiser.
- Worship brings about a spiritual union of God and His People. Lead in Worship.
- Silence is an effective tool in Worship. Do not be afraid to wait on the Lord in silence.
- True Worship will change any atmosphere – anywhere – anytime – for any people. Be a true worshipper.

Chapter 8

THUS LEARN:

- Real success is measured by God's measuring rod alone.
- Trying to impress men will 'mess' you up with God.
- God can do anything, and with Him, success is assured.
- Without God, we can do 'nothing', and our failure is certain.
- Let your expectation be of God, and keep your eyes upon Him.
- No one can beat you at being you, so be the best you that you can be.
- Celebrate the uniqueness of others, in addition to celebrating your own.

Chapter 9

THUS LEARN:

- Souls represent the favorite four-letter word and passion of God.
- The whole Bible is full of Jesus.
- Preach Jesus —His birth, life, death, resurrection and soon return —**the gospel**, for it is the Power of God!
- Preach with the purpose of persuading men and pleasing God.
- There is no greater way to say 'thank you' for all He has done than to proclaim Christ with accuracy, clarity and consistency.
- Preach with the same passion whether it is 2 or 2,000, because God is listening!
- Talk to **Him** before you preach to **them** and never preach without praying for and inviting souls to come to Jesus.
- Celebrate every soul that comes to Jesus, and always Give God the Glory.

Chapter 10

THUS LEARN:

- Ordination originates with God.
- Diligent seeking of God always brings His rewards.
- Faithful service is a pre-requisite for God's promotion.

- You will not have to blow your own horn if you blow His.
- Sincere service and study sets you apart in the eyes of God and Man.
- Seek God's Hand, and in His time, He will add Man's.
- Verse to live by: "But, seek ye first the Kingdom of God, and His righteousness; and all these things shall be added unto you." *Matthew 6:33.*

Chapter 11

THUS LEARN:

- Flexibility enlarges your borders.
- Dependability makes you an asset and not a liability.
- Be sent by Jesus, because if He sends you, you can go 'anywhere' and be OK.
- Keep bouncing back. Do not let offense take up residence in your spirit.
- Trust the Lord to use, and not abuse you.
- You are in Good hands—God's!
- Remember *Jeremiah 29:11, "For I know the thoughts that I think toward you, saith the LORD, thoughts of peace, and not of evil, to give you an expected end."*
- If the telephone does not ring —do not be anxious, be thankful.
- Trust God for your schedule —He knows how much you can bear.

- Enjoy your 'time off', because busy days are ahead.

Chapter 12

THUS LEARN:

- No one is perfect. We all miss God.
- Learn from every mistake and try not to make it again.
- Let the Lord correct and console you.
- Communication is a priceless asset.
- Remember that every invitation may not come from God... always consult Him before going anywhere.
- Keep a record of every time you preach including the date, location, time, message given, manuscript notes, offering received, souls saved and any other comments for future reference and usage.
- Remember, no grabbing.
- Do justly, love mercy and walk humbly with thy God. This is all that God requires, but what He requires counts most. *(Micah 6:8)*

Chapter 13

THUS LEARN:

- Ask God whether you should 'Go' or 'No'.
- Do not be anxious with either answer, because He knows the way that you take.

- Wait for the Lord's release. This will always result in 'increase'.
- Remember that God takes care of His own, full time or not.
- Trust God to know what is best for you, and let Him walk you right into it.

Chapter 14

THUS LEARN:

- Do not ever let them see you sweat —even when you are hot under the collar.
- Do your best, even if others fail their test.
- Guard His name and your reputation as His representative.
- Do not let your good be evil spoken of —guard your words, your walk, and your anointing.
- God doesn't forget your works of righteousness.
- You will reap, if you do not faint.
- No matter what, remember that quitting is not an option.
- While serving people, wait on the Lord. He will sustain you.
- Do your part and "Trust God for the rest.
- Know absolutely that God Will Take Care of you.

Chapter 15

THUS LEARN:

- Whether the lightning is flashing or the thunder is rolling —God has promised never to leave you alone.
- Whether seen or unseen, wherever you go your bodyguards go with you, to cover and protect you from hurt and harm.
- The Lord Himself is with you so that you always have company. Therefore, you do not have to be lonely.
- Knowing that you are 'never' alone does not release you to go just 'anywhere'.
- Obey His voice and only go where God tells you to go.
- Remember, someone would be blessed to hear your bodyguard stories.

Chapter 16

THUS LEARN:

- Time misspent is time lost, and time lost is difficult to regain.
- Time well spent is an invaluable investment that reaps unlimited dividends.
- Time well managed in travel becomes a good friend.
- While traveling, redeem the time: reading, writing, resting and worshiping.

- Walk by faith, but know as much as you can about the trip before you travel.
- Think the trip through as completely as possible.
- Be prepared for the unexpected.
- Take advantage of the travel experience of others.
- Pray without ceasing.
- Praise the Lord for every safe trip.

Chapter 17

THUS LEARN:

- Take time for you —'**me time**' —and do the things that refresh you.
- Let people help you, because it is really help from God.
- Pay for the services that you need and can afford (household maintenance, yard landscaping, hair, cleaning, cooking, etc.).
- Let the skycaps and bellmen lift the bags, and reward them accordingly.
- Get your physical rest, and let your spirit rest in the Lord.
- Drink plenty of water —it is God's medicine.
- Eat right and exercise.
- Believe that you are 'worth it'.
- Don't worry, be happy. Live a full and happy life.
- Do not be afraid to define your needs as a ministry gift.

- Be open to transition and change.
- Stretch without being stressed.

Chapter 18

THUS LEARN:

- Relationships should be inspired by God and initiated as He leads.
- Cultivate your relationships as directed by God.
- Evaluate relationships as signaled by God.
- Good relationships should be cherished and nourished.
- There are great rewards in relationships.
- Friends are special; they keep us in balance.
- Family and friends are essential for emotional health and well-being.
- Thank God for good relationships.

Chapter 19

THUS LEARN:

- Sisters are a gift from God.
- We are family —sisters in the Lord.
- As women, we can change our reputation.
- Servants should not be taken for granted.
- Succourers or benefactors, should be celebrated.
- Be a blessing and you will receive a blessing.

- Be willing to give and receive the help God sends.
- Attire does matter. Listen to God.
- Take good care of Phebe.

Chapter 20

THUS LEARN:

- Recognize the shift in seasons.
- Pay attention so you do not have to pay for ignorance.
- New assignments will come with new and sufficient grace.
- Understand and appreciate your God-given place.
- Serve the flock as a faithful steward.
- Do not be afraid to dream because dreams do come true.
- Never give up on your dreams.
- Real pioneers hold the door open for others.
- Be thankful for and supportive of God-given pioneers.
- You will come full circle.
- Do not forget to be a blessing as you come full circle.

Chapter 21

THUS LEARN:

- Mentoring should be initiated by God.
- No matter what heroes you may have, worship God and don't allow anyone to worship you.
- Mentoring is a process over time.

- Mentoring requires honesty and transparency.
- Mentoring requires spiritual agreement.
- Mentoring does not always equate to friendship.
- Mentoring does not require continuous one on one ministry.
- Observation and spiritual impartation are major mining tools in mentoring.

Chapter 22

THUS LEARN:

- It is very hard to cry over someone else's blessings while counting your own.
- For all that any of us have, a price has been paid —even if it was not paid by us.
- Get busy claiming your own 'stuff' from the Lord, and be thankful.
- Rejoice with others, and someone will always rejoice with you.
- Playtime is over —it never really existed anyway.
- Procrastination should be avoided at all cost, because it costs so much in the end.
- Turn around and look at God.
- Make full proof of your ministry now —you will only get one life to do so.

- The more we study, the more we realize we do not know. And that is a good thing.
- Do not get stuck on good or better, but strive to be your best at all times.
- In crisis, worship God and believe His Word.

CHAPTER 25

FINAL THOUGHTS

Today, more than twenty-five years after embarking upon this preaching journey, in many ways it is even as it was in the beginning. I still look to the Lord for opportunities to preach, and I have more than enough. I still seek Him for His message, and He always has something to say. I am still committed to continued study, that the words of my mouth and the meditation of my heart may be acceptable in His sight, because He is forever my Lord, my strength, and my redeemer.

Today, I find myself worshipping the God of the ages more and more. For, in worship, it is becoming clearer to me that I must work while it is day, because the daylight of my life is slipping away into night, and when night cometh, no man can work. I pray for increased wisdom to know His purpose for me, and believe Him for grace that is sufficient to help me finish my race with patience and great joy.

Likewise, I pray also that something I have shared in this book has been a blessing, and will be helpful to you, as you embrace this high and holy, lofty but weighty, business called preaching.

As I was preparing to enter this year, the Lord gave me instruction to 'search my memory', and pour out the beginning of what I have gleaned in ministry so far. I am certain I will think of something else I could have shared, after this has gone to press. However, God told me to get this first installment into your hands right away. Thus, this offering has been penned for you in this season.

Well beloved, I owe! I owe! So off to preach I go! By plane, train or automobile, I will go! Alone or accompanied, I will go! To storefronts or stadiums, I will go! Please know that I am praying for you, even as I am preparing to 'go again'. And I ask you to pray for me, that until The Lord says enough done, I will continue to fulfill His divine directive that was given to me years ago, to 'Preach, Woman, Preach'! AMEN.

Jesus Christ is Coming Soon!

CLOSING PRAYER

Father, in the name of Jesus, I thank you for all those who read this book, and pray that the lessons and life experiences that are discussed here will be used to build and to edify the body of Christ.

You are the LORD of hosts, the God of Israel, who has revealed to your servant that you will build a house of prayer and praise. With all my heart, I pray for all those who are called to preach the gospel of Jesus Christ. I pray that the eyes of their understanding might be opened, that they may know the hope of their calling, and I pray that they come to a greater understanding of preaching and ministry.

I pray that the house of God be purified. I pray that nothing hinder the truth of the message of Jesus Christ from being taught or preached. I pray that men and women everywhere come to know who Jesus really is so that Your Kingdom can be established in the earth as it is in heaven.

Lord, I pray for those in pulpits around the world. I pray that the name of Jesus be lifted up and that no souls are lost or prevented from coming into the kingdom of God. I pray that hearts may be open toward the House of God night and day, even toward the place of where Your Name is.

Dr. Rita L. Twiggs

I pray that we, as preachers, have no respect of persons in the body of Christ or in the ministry. I pray that the anointing of servanthood will prevail in all churches in this nation and abroad.

I pray that "whosoever will" shall come to know You, Lord, and that souls may spread forth their hands toward the House of God.

Lord, Hallow the House of God, which You have built. Put Your name there forever; and, let all eyes and hearts know that You are there perpetually.

This is my prayer for all those who are called to preach, to teach, and to reach, in Jesus Name. Amen, Amen, and Amen.

Jesus Christ is Coming Soon!

EXCITING MESSAGES BY DR. RITA L. TWIGGS

A GOOD WOMAN IS NOT HARD TO FIND

A WOMAN AND HER GIFT

A WOMAN AND HER INHERITANCE

A WOMAN AND HER MONEY

A WOMAN'S TOUCH

HE'S ABLE

KEEP LAPI HAPPY

NO TRACE OF THE ATTACK

PREACH WOMAN PREACH

SHE-MOTIONS

THE LORD HELPED ME

WHEN WOMEN SPEAK

WOMEN IN MINISTRY

For other available products and engagement information, please sign on to the website WWW.RITATWIGGS.ORG.

Send Engagement Request to:

Rita Twiggs Ministries
P.O. Box 64223
Washington, DC 20029
Fax: 202-398-6770